STEP UP 成长 with CHINESE

WORKBOOK 2

主编： 崔希亮
Series Editor　Xiliang Cui

北京语言大学 Beijing Language & Culture University:

编者： 陈丽霞　张兰欣　徐式婧　李耘达
Writers　Lixia Chen　Lanxin Zhang　Shijing Xu　Yunda Li

美国教育专家 American Educators:

陈少元　陶洁琳　竹露茜　李艳惠
Carol Chen-Lin　Janice Dowd　Lucy Chu Lee　Yen-hui Audrey Li

谭大立　赵丹
Dali Tan　Dan Zhao

CENGAGE Learning

Andover • Melbourne • Mexico City • Boston, MA • Toronto • Hong Kong • New Delhi • Seoul • Singapore • Tokyo

CENGAGE Learning

Step Up with Chinese Workbook 2

Publishing Director:
Roy Lee

Editorial Manager, CLT:
Zhao Lan

Associate Development Editor:
Titus Teo

Creative Manager:
Melvin Chong

Senior Product Manager (Asia):
Joyce Tan

Product Manager (Outside Asia):
Mei Yun Loh

Regional Manager, Production and Rights:
Pauline Lim

Senior Production Executive:
Cindy Chai

Senior Project Executive (China):
Mana Wu

Compositor:
Hwee Suan Yap

© 2014 Cengage Learning Asia Pte Ltd

ALL RIGHTS RESERVED. No part of this work covered by the copyright herein may be reproduced, transmitted, stored or used in any form or by any means graphic, electronic, or mechanical, including but not limited to photocopying, recording, scanning, digitalizing, taping, Web distribution, information networks, or information storage and retrieval systems, without the prior written permission of the publisher.

For product information and technology assistance, contact us at
Cengage Learning Asia Customer Support, 65-6410-1200

For permission to use material from this text or product,
submit all requests online at **www.cengageasia.com/permissions**
Further permissions questions can be emailed to
asia.permissionrequest@cengage.com

ISBN-13: 978-981-4455-18-3
ISBN-10: 981-4455-18-0

Cengage Learning Asia Pte Ltd
151 Lorong Chuan
#02-08 New Tech Park
Singapore 556741

Cengage Learning is a leading provider of customized learning solutions with office locations around the globe, including Andover, Melbourne, Mexico City, Boston (MA), Toronto, Hong Kong, New Delhi, Seoul, Singapore and Tokyo. Locate your local office at **www.cengage.com/global**

Cengage Learning products are represented in Canada by Nelson Education, Ltd.

For information on our Chinese language teaching products, visit **www.cengagechinese.com**

Visit our Asia website at **www.cengageasia.com**

Every reasonable effort has been made to acquire permission for copyright material in this text, and to acknowledge such indebtedness accurately. Any errors or omissions called to the publisher's attention will be corrected in future printing.

Photo Credits:

Cover: Yukmin/Asia Images/Getty Images

Pages: **20** (t to b) Digital Vision/Thinkstock, iStockphoto/Thinkstock, iStockphoto/Thinkstock, Pixland/Thinkstock; **21** (t to b) iStockphoto/Thinkstock, iStockphoto/Thinkstock, Jupiterimages/Photos.com/Thinkstock; **25** (l to r, t to b) Thinkstock Images/Comstock/Thinkstock, iStockphoto/Thinkstock, Jupiterimages/Comstock/Thinkstock, Digital Vision/Thinkstock, Hemera/Thinkstock, Creatas/Thinkstock, Creatas/Thinkstock; **46** (l to r) iStockphoto/Thinkstock, iStockphoto/Thinkstock; **48** iStockphoto/Thinkstock; **78** (l to r, t to b) iStockphoto/Thinkstock, iStockphoto/Thinkstock, iStockphoto/Thinkstock, iStockphoto/Thinkstock; **80** (l to r) iStockphoto/Thinkstock, Creatas/Thinkstock, Chris Clinton/Lifesize/Thinkstock; **81** iStockphoto/Thinkstock; **114** (l to r, t to b) iStockphoto/Thinkstock, Hemera/Thinkstock, iStockphoto/Thinkstock, iStockphoto/Thinkstock, Fuse/Thinkstock, Creatas Images/Creatas/Thinkstock, iStockphoto/Thinkstock, Fuse/Thinkstock; **117** (l to r) iStockphoto/Thinkstock, iStockphoto/Thinkstock, iStockphoto/Thinkstock; **118** (l to r) Digital Vision/Thinkstock, iStockphoto/Thinkstock, iStockphoto/Thinkstock; **167** (t to b) iStockphoto/Thinkstock, iStockphoto/Thinkstock; **168** (t to b) Zoonar/Thinkstock, Blend Images/Thinkstock, iStockphoto/Thinkstock; **202** (l to r, t to b) iStockphoto/Thinkstock, iStockphoto/Thinkstock, iStockphoto/Thinkstock, iStockphoto/Thinkstock, iStockphoto/Thinkstock

Printed in Singapore
2 3 4 5 17 16 15

Table of Contents

Lesson 1	Starting a new school year	1
Lesson 2	Moving to a new school	23
Lesson 3	Settling into a new home	45
Lesson 4	Adapting to the weather	65
Lesson 5	Discovering the community	83
REVIEW 1	(Lessons 1-5)	103
Lesson 6	Meeting new people	113
Lesson 7	Maintaining a healthy lifestyle	132
Lesson 8	Connecting with others	153
Lesson 9	Getting along with others	174
Lesson 10	Being a global citizen	194
REVIEW 2	(Lessons 6-10)	216

LESSON 1: STARTING A NEW SCHOOL YEAR

STEP 1 MEETING AND GREETING PEOPLE

Listening

1. Listening rejoinder. Listen to the question and choose the correct response.
   - Ⓐ 不忙！你呢？
   - Ⓑ 明天见！
   - Ⓒ 很累。
   - Ⓓ 没有。   (   )

2. Listening rejoinder. Listen to the question and choose the correct response.
   - Ⓐ 不是。
   - Ⓑ 很好，谢谢！
   - Ⓒ 你呢？
   - Ⓓ 很高兴认识你！   (   )

3. Listening rejoinder. Listen to the statement and choose the correct response.
   - Ⓐ 你很高。
   - Ⓑ 你家在中国吗？
   - Ⓒ 我也是！
   - Ⓓ 你呢？   (   )

4. Listening rejoinder. Listen to the statement and choose the correct question to the statement.
   - Ⓐ 今天星期几？
   - Ⓑ 你喜欢吃饺子，对吗？
   - Ⓒ 我喝茶，你呢？
   - Ⓓ 今天我们吃饺子，好吗？   (   )

5. Listening rejoinder. Listen to the question and choose the correct response.
   - Ⓐ 我爸爸住在日本。
   - Ⓑ 今天是我的生日。
   - Ⓒ 很忙，也很累。
   - Ⓓ 她八点上课。   (   )

6. Listening rejoinder. Listen to the statement and choose the correct response.
   - Ⓐ 一会儿！   Ⓑ 你好！   Ⓒ 你怎么样？   Ⓓ 明天见！   (   )

Speaking

1. How do you greet your classmate in the following situations?
   1) Meeting each other on the first day of school after summer vacation.
   2) Meeting each other for the very first time.
   3) Before you leave for home after school on Monday.
   4) As you leave for a class that you two do not share.

2. Ask and answer questions with a partner using the "verb+不+verb" or "adjective+不+adjective" structure to find out whether
   1) today is Friday.
   2) his/her friend likes fish.
   3) his/her parents live in New York.
   4) his/her classmate is busy.

3. Create five questions for your partner using 吗 to get to know your new teacher.

   Example: 老师是美国人吗？

4. How do you find out your friend's daily schedule using tag questions? Make five sentences using tag questions.

   Example: 你早上七点起床，是吗？

Reading

1. Match the following greetings with the appropriate situations.

   1) 明天见！   A) You haven't see each other for a month.
   2) 早上好！   B) You head to a meeting while your friend goes to a class.
   3) 好久不见！你好吗？ C) You haven't seen a friend recently.
   4) 你最近怎么样？   D) 7:00 a.m.
   5) 一会儿见！   E) You are about to leave for home after school.

STEP UP WITH CHINESE 2

2. Read the following speech and determine whether the statements below are true (T) or false (F).

> "欢迎回来！你们的暑假过得好不好？我是你们的中文老师，我姓高，我叫高文英。很高兴认识你们！"

1) The speaker will be teaching the listeners. ( )
2) The listeners are learning English. ( )
3) The speech happens on the last day of school before summer. ( )
4) The speaker and the listeners do not know each other before this event. ( )

3. Read the dialog and choose the best answer to each question.

高老师：你好，王明！好久不见，你怎么样？

王　明：您好，高老师！我很好！您呢？您最近好不好？

高老师：我也很好，只是(zhǐshì / just that)很忙，明天是9月1号，开学(kāixué / school opens)的第一天。是最忙的一天。

王　明：您的暑假过得怎么样？

高老师：我的暑假过得很好！我每天游泳、打篮球。你呢？

王　明：我的暑假也不错。我在中国玩了一个月，去(qù / go)了北京、上海，还有香港。对了，中午我们一起(yìqǐ / together)吃饭，好不好？我给您看我在中国的照片(zhàopiàn / photos)。

高老师：我今天中午有个会(huì / meeting)，明天中午好吗？

王　明：好！明天中午十二点，在学校餐厅！

高老师：好！明天中午见！

王　明：明天见！

LESSON 1 STARTING A NEW SCHOOL YEAR

1) 今天是几月几号？
   - Ⓐ 八月二十九号
   - Ⓑ 九月一号
   - Ⓒ 八月三十一号
   - Ⓓ 五月三十号   (   )

2) 高老师最近怎么样？
   - Ⓐ 很忙
   - Ⓑ 很累
   - Ⓒ 很好
   - Ⓓ 很高兴   (   )

3) 高老师和王明要在哪一天一起吃午饭？
   - Ⓐ 今天
   - Ⓑ 明天
   - Ⓒ 后天
   - Ⓓ 大后天   (   )

4) 高老师今天中午要做什么？
   - Ⓐ 他要上课。
   - Ⓑ 他要去中国。
   - Ⓒ 他要开会。
   - Ⓓ 他要和小王吃饭。   (   )

4. Answer the following questions based on your personal life and preferences.

   1) 你喜欢不喜欢喝绿茶？ _____

   2) 你晚上十一点睡觉，是吗？ _____

   3) 你有没有宠物？ _____

   4) 你属不属虎？ _____

   5) 你的同学们住在学校，是吗？ _____

   6) 你的好朋友喜欢不喜欢吃中国菜？ _____

Writing

1. Practice writing the following characters in the correct stroke order.

久 久 久 久

兴 兴 兴 兴 兴 兴 兴

暑 暑 暑 暑 暑 暑 暑 暑 暑 暑 暑 暑
假 假 假 假 假 假 假 假 假 假 假

暑假　暑假　暑假

欢 欢 欢 欢 欢 欢
迎 迎 迎 迎 迎 迎 迎

欢迎　欢迎　欢迎

回 回 回 回 回 回
来 来 来 来 来 来 来

回来　回来　回来

认 认 认 认
识 识 识 识 识 识 识

认识　认识　认识

LESSON 1 STARTING A NEW SCHOOL YEAR

2. Write your greetings for the following situations.
   1) You meet a new friend.

   _____

   2) You meet an old friend after a long time.

   _____

   3) You welcome your classmates back to school.

   _____

   4) You say "good-bye" to your classmates after your first class.

   _____

   5) You say "good-bye" to your classmates on Friday afternoon before heading home.

   _____

3. You have not written to a friend recently. How do you start your email to find out how your friend has been doing?

   _____

   _____

   _____

4. What would you propose to your best friend to do on the following days? Use 好吗 to form tag questions.

   1) 七月四号 _____

   2) 二月十四号 _____

   3) 一月一号 _____

4) 四月一号 _____

5) 十月三十一号 _____

6) 他/她的生日 _____

5. This is a pair guessing game. First you need to write down a classmate's name as your secret pen pal. Then by asking yes-no questions, you are to find out your partner's secret pen pal. Write 10 yes-no questions to ask your partner.

Example: 你的朋友是不是男孩？

_____

_____

_____

_____

_____

_____

_____

STEP 2　TELLING THE DAY AND TIME

Listening

1. Listening rejoinder. Listen to the question and choose the correct response.
   - Ⓐ 礼拜一
   - Ⓑ 礼拜天
   - Ⓒ 礼拜六
   - Ⓓ 礼拜四　　　　　　　　　　　　　　　　　　（　　）

2. Listening rejoinder. Listen to the question and choose the correct response.
   - Ⓐ 我下午三点放学。
   - Ⓑ 我明天上中文课。
   - Ⓒ 我周末看电影了。
   - Ⓓ 我下个星期放暑假。　　　　　　　　　　　　（　　）

3. Listen to the statement and then the question in English. Choose the correct answer.
   QUESTION: When is the second semester?
   - Ⓐ 九月到一月
   - Ⓑ 九月到二月
   - Ⓒ 一月到五月
   - Ⓓ 一月到六月　　　　　　　　　　　　　　　　（　　）

4. Listen to Mary's schedule and then the question in English. Choose the correct answer.
   QUESTION: What is the correct order of Mary's evening activities?
   - Ⓐ 吃饭，看电视，睡觉，做功课
   - Ⓑ 做功课，吃饭，看电视，睡觉
   - Ⓒ 吃饭，看电视，做功课，睡觉
   - Ⓓ 睡觉，做功课，看电视，吃饭　　　　　　　　（　　）

5. Listen to David's schedule and then the question in English. Choose the correct answer.
   QUESTION: What class does David have before Chinese class every Monday?
   - Ⓐ 英文
   - Ⓑ 数学
   - Ⓒ 历史
   - Ⓓ 中文　　　　　　　　　　　　　　　　　　　（　　）

Speaking

1. Imagine today is Wednesday. Work in pairs to ask and answer questions on the days of the week using 礼拜 or 周.

    Example: 昨天是周几？昨天是周二。

2. What do you do before going to bed on weekdays? Create three sentences using 以前.

3. What do you do after school on Wednesdays? Create three sentences using 以后.

4. Work in pairs to ask and answer questions about your partner's daily schedule. Put what you have found in a table, including a column for time and a column for activities. List at least eight activities.

Reading

1. Match the day and the date accordingly.

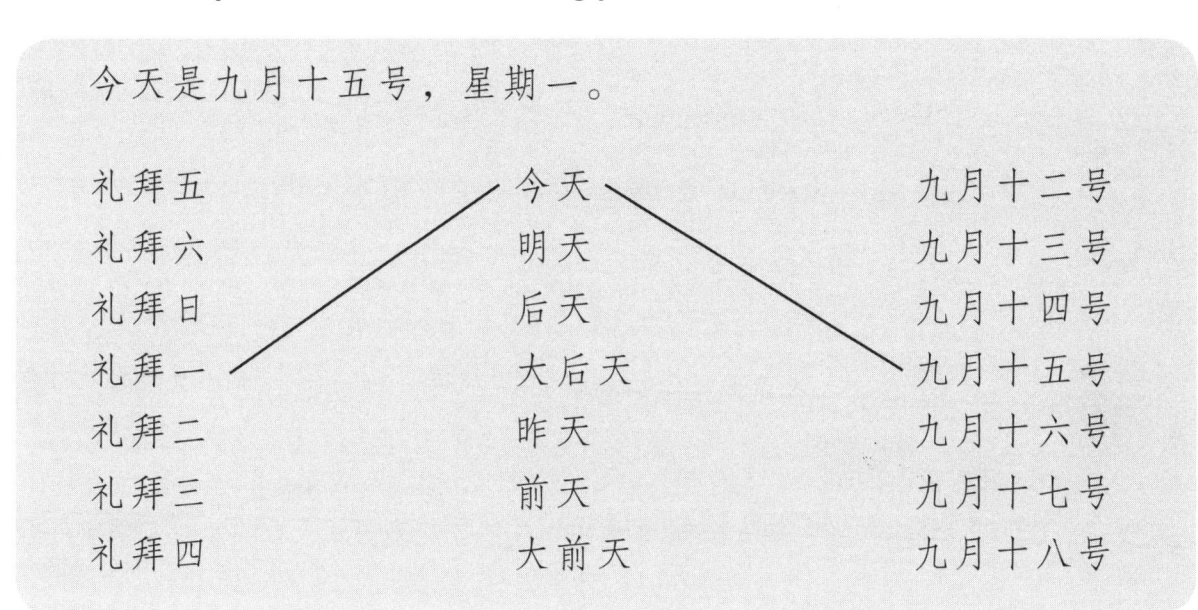

   今天是九月十五号，星期一。

礼拜五	今天	九月十二号
礼拜六	明天	九月十三号
礼拜日	后天	九月十四号
礼拜一	大后天	九月十五号
礼拜二	昨天	九月十六号
礼拜三	前天	九月十七号
礼拜四	大前天	九月十八号

2. Choose the most appropriate answer for each of the questions below.

   Ⓐ 周一　　Ⓑ 周二　　Ⓒ 周三　　Ⓓ 周四
   Ⓔ 周五　　Ⓕ 周六　　Ⓖ 周日

   1) 周一以前是周几？　　　　　　　　　　　　　　　　　(　　)
   2) 周六以后是周几？　　　　　　　　　　　　　　　　　(　　)

LESSON 1 STARTING A NEW SCHOOL YEAR

3) 周末是周几和周几？ (   )
4) 一周的第一天是周几？ (   )
5) 一周的第四天是周几？ (   )
6) 一周的第七天是周几？ (   )
7) 你最喜欢周几？ (   )
8) 你最不喜欢周几？ (   )

3. Read the dialog and answer the questions.

芳芳：明天星期六了，你这个周末做什么？

安琪：我星期六想去打球，你也来打球，好吗？
　　　　　　　　　　　　　come

芳芳：我很喜欢打球，你几点去？打多久？

安琪：我上午九点去，从九点到十一点都在体育馆。

芳芳：哎呀，我星期六八点起床，八点半吃饭，吃饭以后
　　　āiyā
　　　expressing surprise
　　　上网、看书，还要做作业。

安琪：你周末也太忙了！礼拜天你有时间吗？我们想看
　　　　　　　　tài
　　　　　　　　too
　　　　　　　　　　　　bùnéngshǎo
　　　电影《一个都不能少》。
　　　　　　　　　　cannot miss
　　　　　　　　　　tīngshuō
芳芳：我没看过这个电影，听说很好！你们在哪儿看？几点？
　　　　　　　　　　　　heard that
　　　　　　　　　　　　　　　　　　　　　　　　　　　bɑ
安琪：下午六点，在我家，我的朋友们也来。你也来吧！
　　　　　　　　　　　　　　　　　　　　　　(indicating a
　　　　　　　　　　　　　　　　　　　　　　suggestion)

芳芳：太好了！谢谢！周日见！

安琪：周日见！

1) 安琪什么时候去打球？
   Ⓐ 周六上午   Ⓑ 周日下午
   Ⓒ 周六下午   Ⓓ 周日下午   (   )

2) 安琪从几点到几点在体育馆?
   Ⓐ 九点到十点　　　　　　Ⓑ 九点到十一点
   Ⓒ 十一点到十二点　　　　Ⓓ 十点到十二点　　　　（　　）

3) 芳芳周六要做什么?
   Ⓐ 上网、看书、做作业
   Ⓑ 上网、看书、打篮球
   Ⓒ 上网、打篮球、看电影
   Ⓓ 上网、看电视、看书　　　　　　　　　　　　（　　）

4) 芳芳周日做什么?
   Ⓐ 去安琪家看电影
   Ⓑ 在家里看电视
   Ⓒ 去体育馆打球
   Ⓓ 在家里做作业　　　　　　　　　　　　　　　（　　）

4. Read the following passage and determine whether the statements below are true (T) or false (F).

我最喜欢的城市(chéngshì city)是中国的北京。北京在中国的北方。这里有好吃的中国菜，还有友好(yǒuhǎo friendly)的人们。这里一年有四季，春天是从三月到五月，夏天是从六月到八月，秋天是从九月到十一月，从十二月到二月是冬天。九月是北京最美(měi beautiful)的时候，也是北京最舒服(shūfu comfortable)的时候。学校九月开学。学校一年有两个学期，秋季学期和冬季学期。每个星期，从星期一到星期五，学生们都很忙。周末是最轻松(qīngsōng relaxed)、最快乐(kuàilè happy)的时候。他们喜欢和朋友看电视、看电影，也喜欢上网、打电脑游戏。我在北京住了十多年了。我家人和我都喜欢北京。

LESSON 1 STARTING A NEW SCHOOL YEAR

1) 北京的八月是夏天。 （　　）
2) 北京的二月是春天。 （　　）
3) 北京的学生周六和周日不太忙。 （　　）
4) 北京最好的时候是在九月。 （　　）
5) 北京的学生不喜欢上网、打电脑游戏。 （　　）
6) 北京在中国的南方。 （　　）

Writing

1. Practice writing the following characters in the correct stroke order.

礼礼礼礼礼
拜拜拜拜拜拜拜拜拜

礼拜

周周周周周周周周
末末末末末

周末

时时时时时时
候候候候候候候候候

时候

考考考考考考
试试试试试试试试

考试

2. Answer the questions based on your personal life.

1) 你秋天什么时候开学？
   _____

2) 你秋天学期什么时候期中考试？
   _____

3) 你一年有几个学期？都是什么学期？
   _____

4) 你什么时候放暑假？
   _____

5) 暑假从几月到几月？
   _____

6) 春假从几月到几月？
   _____

3. Fill in the blanks using 以前 or 以后.

   十二生肖有鼠、牛、虎、兔、龙、蛇、马、羊、猴、鸡、狗和猪。鼠年（_____）是牛年。兔年（_____）是虎年。2013年是蛇年，蛇年（_____）是马年，蛇年（_____）是龙年。你属什么？是哪年出生的？

LESSON 1 STARTING A NEW SCHOOL YEAR

4. Write down your Monday schedule; then write an essay of at least 10 sentences describing your day.

Example: 第一节课	英文	从 8:00 到 8:45

You may begin like this: 星期一是我最忙的一天……

_____

_____

_____

_____

_____

_____

_____

STEP 3 DESCRIBING YOUR SUMMER VACATION

Listening

1. Listen to the dialog and then the question in English. Choose the correct answer.
   QUESTION: How long did Fangfang stay in Beijing?
   - Ⓐ 三个月
   - Ⓑ 四个月
   - Ⓒ 两个月
   - Ⓓ 五个月   (   )

2. Listening rejoinder. Listen to the question and choose the correct response.
   - Ⓐ 我不是。
   - Ⓑ 我不参加。
   - Ⓒ 我没参加。
   - Ⓓ 我要参加。   (   )

3. Listen to the dialog and then the question in English. Choose the correct answer
   QUESTION: What does Mark like to do?
   - Ⓐ 呆在家里
   - Ⓑ 去海边
   - Ⓒ 做作业
   - Ⓓ 睡觉   (   )

4. Listening rejoinder. Listen to the question and choose the correct response.
   - Ⓐ 我的中文不好。
   - Ⓑ 我过得很有意思。
   - Ⓒ 我觉得很紧张。
   - Ⓓ 我感到开心极了。   (   )

Speaking

1. For each of the following situations, provide a response by creating a sentence describing how you would feel.
   1) You are meeting your pen pal later.
   2) Your teacher assigned no homework today.
   3) You will have an interview for selecting candidates to study in China.
   4) Your favorite athlete is hurt in a game.
   5) You see people waste food.
   6) You receive a gift that you have been expecting.

2. Work in pairs. Each person writes down six activities you did during summer vacation. One activity is true, and the other five are false. Try to find out which is the true activity your partner did by asking questions.

   Example: 你暑假参加夏令营了吗？

3. Share with a partner one of your favorite vacations and one of your least favorite vacations. Share what you did during the vacation as well.

   Example: 我去年暑假过得开心极了！我去地中海旅游了，还参加很好玩的音乐夏令营。

Reading

1. Read the brief introduction of each person and match them with an activity.

   A 做义工 **B** 参加夏令营
   C 打工   **D** 上补习班
   E 呆在家里 **F** 逛街
   G 去海边

   1) 芳芳喜欢交朋友，也喜欢学新东西，她不喜欢买东西。   (   )
      jiāo   dōngxi
      befriend   things

   2) 安琪明年要去中国旅游，她要赚钱，买机票。   (   )
      zhuàn qián   jīpiào
      earn money   air tickets

   3) 玛丽喜欢买东西。   (   )

   4) 小伟不喜欢出去玩。   (   )
      chūqu
      go out

   5) 马克喜欢帮人。   (   )
      bāng
      help

   6) 张安的英语不好，他想在暑假学英语。   (   )

   7) 丁强喜欢大海。   (   )
      dà
      big

2. Choose the best option that matches the description.

1) 六月我去上数学补习班，每天从早上八点到下午三点都在学校。放学后，也有很多功课，每个星期五还要考试。我不喜欢数学。你觉得六月我过得怎么样？
   - Ⓐ 开心极了
   - Ⓑ 无聊极了
   - Ⓒ 伤心极了
   - Ⓓ 兴奋极了   (   )

2) 暑假我要去北极旅游。我感到＿＿＿＿＿极了！
   Běijí / Arctic
   - Ⓐ 难过
   - Ⓑ 生气
   - Ⓒ 紧张
   - Ⓓ 兴奋   (   )

3) ＿＿＿＿＿＿＿＿＿＿＿＿＿＿＿＿＿，因为我们有一个中文考试。
   yīnwèi / because
   - Ⓐ 我昨天晚上看电影了
   - Ⓑ 我昨天晚上和朋友打电脑游戏了
   - Ⓒ 我昨天晚上去老师那里补习中文了
   - Ⓓ 我昨天晚上去看棒球比赛了   (   )

4) ＿＿＿＿＿＿＿＿＿＿＿＿＿＿＿＿＿，因为我在小学做义工了。
   xiǎo / elementary school
   - Ⓐ 今年暑假我上暑期学校了
   - Ⓑ 今年暑假我过得很开心
   - Ⓒ 今年暑假我没有参加夏令营
   - Ⓓ 我觉得今年暑假过得很有意义   (   )

3. Answer the following questions based on your life last summer.

1) 你打工了吗？＿＿＿＿＿＿＿＿＿＿＿＿＿＿＿＿＿＿＿＿＿＿＿＿＿＿

2) 你参加夏令营了吗？＿＿＿＿＿＿＿＿＿＿＿＿＿＿＿＿＿＿＿＿＿＿

3) 你看电影了吗？＿＿＿＿＿＿＿＿＿＿＿＿＿＿＿＿＿＿＿＿＿＿＿＿

4) 你逛街了吗？＿＿＿＿＿＿＿＿＿＿＿＿＿＿＿＿＿＿＿＿＿＿＿＿＿

5) 你去海边了吗？＿＿＿＿＿＿＿＿＿＿＿＿＿＿＿＿＿＿＿＿＿＿＿＿

6) 你做义工了吗？＿＿＿＿＿＿＿＿＿＿＿＿＿＿＿＿＿＿＿＿＿＿＿＿

7) 你出国旅游了吗？＿＿＿＿＿＿＿＿＿＿＿＿＿＿＿＿＿＿＿＿＿＿＿

8) 你参加补习班了吗？＿＿＿＿＿＿＿＿＿＿＿＿＿＿＿＿＿＿＿＿＿＿

4. Read the dialog and determine whether the following statements are true (T) or false (F).

张安：马克，今天星期五，你放学以后去看电影吗？

马克：去啊，我们一起去吧？

张安：我今天不去了，我昨天没有游泳，今天想去游泳。你昨天游泳了吗？

马克：我也没游泳。今天有篮球赛(sài competition)，我昨天八点就(jiù as soon as)睡觉了。

张安：哦，今天的篮球赛怎么样？

马克：我们赢(yíng win)了，大家(dàjiā all of us)都开心极了。

张安：太好了！对了，上周六下午，你们几个人去了海边了吗，怎么样？好玩吗？

马克：上周六天气(tiānqì weather)不好，我们没有去海边，都呆在我家。无聊极了。

张安：哦，时间不早了，我要上中文课了！再见！

马克：好，再见！周末快乐！

1) 马克昨天游泳了。 ( )
2) 张安昨天游泳了。 ( )
3) 马克上周六没有去海边。 ( )
4) 张安今天看篮球赛了。 ( )
5) 马克和张安今天下课以后要去看电影。 ( )
6) 明天是星期六。 ( )

Writing

1. Practice writing the following characters in the correct stroke order.

参 参 参 参 参 参 参 参
加 加 加 加 加

参加 | 参加 | 参加 | | |

去 去 去 去 去

去 | 去 | 去 | 去 | | | | | |

呆 呆 呆 呆 呆 呆 呆

呆 | 呆 | 呆 | 呆 | | | | | |

买 买 买 买 买 买

买 | 买 | 买 | 买 | | | | | |

逛 逛 逛 逛 逛 逛 逛 逛

逛 | 逛 | 逛 | 逛 | | | | |

开 开 开 开
心 心 心 心

开心 | 开心 | 开心 | | |

LESSON 1 STARTING A NEW SCHOOL YEAR

觉 觉觉觉觉觉觉觉觉觉

感 感感感感感感感感感感感

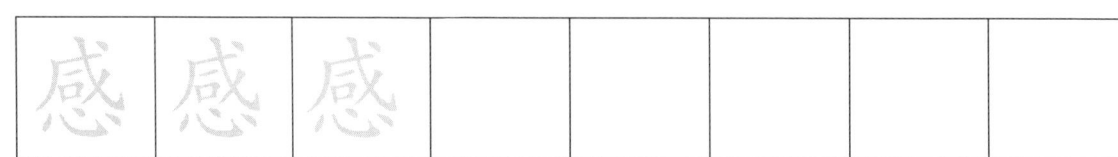

2. Describe the following pictures in Chinese using one sentence that describes the person's emotions.

1)

2)

3)

4)

STEP UP WITH CHINESE 2

5) _____

6) _____

7) _____

3. Write a sentence to tell what you had already done by the time listed below on Mondays.

1) 8:40 am _____

2) 1:15 pm _____

3) 4:40 pm _____

4) 7:00 pm _____

5) 11:00 pm _____

LESSON 1 STARTING A NEW SCHOOL YEAR

4. Write an email to your Chinese e-pal describing your summer vacation, talking about where you went and what you did. Ask him/her some questions about his/her summer. Make sure to use 了, 从…到, 也, 还, and 都 in some of the sentences. Write at least 10 sentences.

LESSON 2 — MOVING TO A NEW SCHOOL

STEP 1 GOING TO PLACES

Listening

1. Mary is talking about the modes of transportation she uses in Beijing. Check the modes of transportation you hear.

   A 公交车　　（　　）　　　　B 自行车　　（　　）
   C 地铁　　　（　　）　　　　D 飞机　　　（　　）
   E 出租车　　（　　）　　　　F 火车　　　（　　）
   G 船　　　　（　　）

2. Listen to the dialog and then the question in English. Choose the correct answer.
   QUESTION: How did Lily's father go to work today?

   A 坐地铁　　　　　　　　　B 坐公交车
   C 骑自行车　　　　　　　　D 开车　　　　　　　　　（　　）

3. Listening rejoinder. Listen to the question and choose the correct response.

   A 我是坐火车去的。
   B 是去年一月去的。
   C 我是从北京去的。
   D 我去年去纽约参加一个夏令营。　　　　　　　　　（　　）

4. Listen to the dialog and then the question in English. Choose the correct answer.
   QUESTION: How does Mark go to school?

   A 坐地铁　　　　　　　　　B 坐公共汽车
   C 坐爸爸的车　　　　　　　D 开车　　　　　　　　　（　　）

5. Listen to the dialog and then the question in English. Choose the correct answer.
   QUESTION: Where is Anqi going tomorrow? Which mode of transportation will she be taking?

   A 上海；坐火车　　　　　　B 上海；坐飞机
   C 北京；坐出租车　　　　　D 北京；骑自行车　　　　（　　）

Speaking

1. State the modes of transportation available in the place where you live.

2. How would you travel to the following places based on the given distance?

School	Zoo	Library	Gym	Airport	Dining hall
2 miles away	10 miles away	500 feet away	100 feet away	50 miles away	50 feet away

3. What are the transportation options to travel to the following places from your location?
    1) New York
    2) Cairo
    3) Los Angeles
    4) Beijing
    5) London
    6) Boston
    7) Your school
    8) Alaska
    9) Rio de Janeiro, Brazil
    10) Sydney, Australia

4. Work with a partner to talk about a trip you took, a meal you had, or a movie you watched this past summer. Take turns to ask and answer questions on when the event took place, how you got there, and who went with you. Use the 是…的 construction in your questions and answers.

Reading

1. Match the words with the correct pictures.

   1) 骑自行车　　　　　(　　)　　5) 走路　　　　　　　(　　)
   2) 坐出租车　　　　　(　　)　　6) 开车　　　　　　　(　　)
   3) 坐船　　　　　　　(　　)　　7) 坐火车　　　　　　(　　)
   4) 坐飞机　　　　　　(　　)

2. Read Mark's after-school schedule and number the following sentences in the correct order from Monday to Sunday.

	星期一	星期二	星期三	星期四	星期五	星期六	星期天
Location	体育馆	操场	图书馆	家里	同学的家	海边	电影院
Activity	打篮球	踢足球	看书	打电动	生日	游泳	看电影
Transport taken	地铁	爸爸的车	公交车	地铁	地铁	妈妈的车	妈妈的车

(　　) 马克坐地铁去同学家。
(　　) 马克坐爸爸的车去操场。
(　　) 马克坐妈妈的车去电影院。
(　　) 马克坐地铁去体育馆。
(　　) 马克坐公交车去图书馆。
(　　) 马克坐妈妈的车去海边。
(　　) 马克坐地铁回家。

3. Read the following email and determine whether the following sentences are true (T) or false (F).

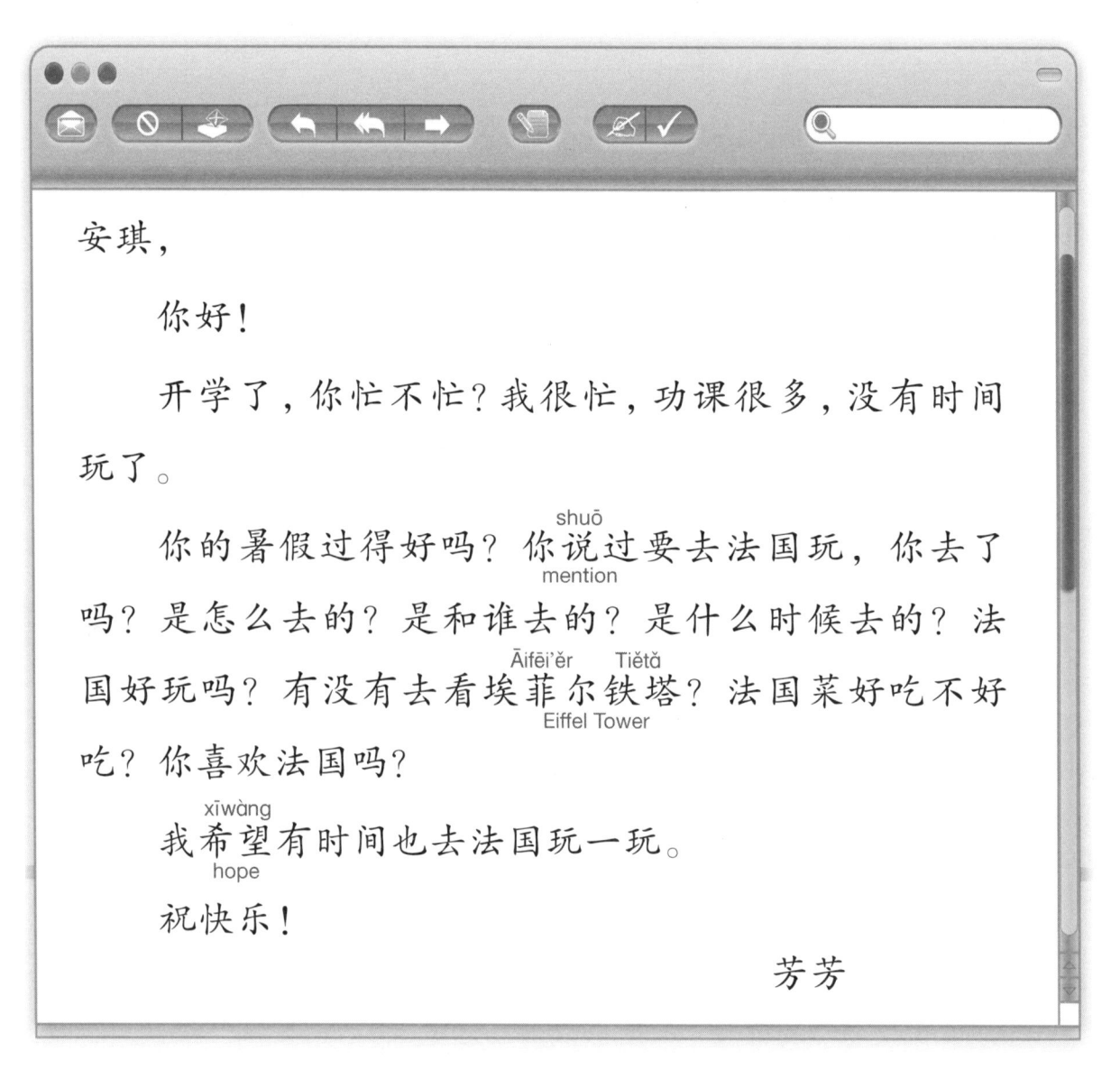

安琪，

你好！

开学了，你忙不忙？我很忙，功课很多，没有时间玩了。

你的暑假过得好吗？你说过要去法国玩，你去了吗？是怎么去的？是和谁去的？是什么时候去的？法国好玩吗？有没有去看埃菲尔铁塔？法国菜好吃不好吃？你喜欢法国吗？

我希望有时间也去法国玩一玩。

祝快乐！

芳芳

---

shuō — mention
Āifēi'ěr Tiětǎ — Eiffel Tower
xīwàng — hope

1) 安琪是学生。　　　　　　　　　　　　　　　　　　　　　　　　(　　)

2) 芳芳没有去过法国。　　　　　　　　　　　　　　　　　　　　　(　　)

3) 芳芳不知道安琪暑假有没有去法国。　　　　　　　　　　　　　　(　　)
   zhīdào — know

4) 芳芳不想去法国，因为她很忙。　　　　　　　　　　　　　　　　(　　)

4. Read the message and answer the questions in Chinese.   是…的?

芳芳：

　　妈妈今天很忙，下班以后要开会(kāihuì have a meeting)，不能(bù néng cannot)来接你。下午三点半李阿姨会(huì will)来。她接你以后，会去弟弟的学校接他，然后(ránhòu then)一起(yìqǐ together)回家。她的车是白色的。她的电话(diànhuà phone number)是235 443 8877。晚上爸爸从纽约回来以后，我们一起去吃上海菜。

　　　　　　　　　　　　　　　　　妈妈

1) Who will be picking Fangfang up today?

_____

2) Why is Fangfang's mother unable to pick her up?

_____

3) What time do Fangfang's classes end?

_____

4) Do Fangfang and her brother go to the same school?

_____

5) Where will Fangfang and her family go tonight?

_____

LESSON 2 MOVING TO A NEW SCHOOL

Writing

1. Practice writing the following characters in the correct stroke order.

来 来 来 来 来 来 来

去 去 去 去 去

坐 坐 坐 坐 坐 坐 坐

走 走 走 走 走 走

骑 骑 骑 骑 骑 骑 骑 骑 骑 骑

回 回 回 回 回 回

送 送 送 送 送 送 送 送 送

接　接　接　接　接　接　接　接　接　接　接
接
接　接　接

2. Rank all modes of transportation you have learned by their speed from the slowest to the fastest.

走路，_____，_____，

_____，_____，

_____，_____，

_____，_____，

_____，坐飞机。

3. Fill in the blanks for Fangfang's thank-you note to her mother, including driving her to school daily, picking her up from school daily, and three other sentences.

qīn'ài
亲爱的妈妈，
dear

谢谢您给我的爱！

妈妈谢谢您 _____。

妈妈谢谢您 _____。

妈妈谢谢您 _____。

妈妈谢谢您 _____。

妈妈谢谢您 _____。

爱你的芳芳

LESSON 2 MOVING TO A NEW SCHOOL

4. Search online and find out how you can travel to the Forbidden City in Beijing from your home. Then list your plan for the modes of transportation.

   Step 1: 坐爸爸的车去机场

   Step 2: _____

   Step 3: _____

   Step 4: _____

   Step 5: _____

5. Write a reply email based on Question 3 in the earlier Reading section. Tell Fangfang one of your travel experiences in detail, including where you went, how you went, with whom you went, and what happened there.

STEP 2 MOVING TO A NEW PLACE

Listening

1. Listen to the dialog and then the question in English. Choose the correct answer.
   QUESTION: Which two cities are separated by 12 hours by air?
   - Ⓐ 北京－上海
   - Ⓑ 纽约－上海
   - Ⓒ 北京－香港
   - Ⓓ 纽约－北京   (   )

2. Listen to the recording and then the question in English. Choose the correct answer.
   QUESTION: Why does the person want to move from the city to the suburbs?
   - Ⓐ 城里很方便。
   - Ⓑ 郊区不方便。
   - Ⓒ 郊区离学校很近。
   - Ⓓ 城里很吵，郊区很安静。   (   )

3. Listening rejoinder. Listen to the question and choose the most appropriate response to follow.
   - Ⓐ 我的爸爸妈妈是一九八七年来美国的。
   - Ⓑ 我的爷爷奶奶是坐船从英国来美国的。
   - Ⓒ 我的外公外婆是从中国来的。
   - Ⓓ 我的爸爸妈妈是去年去美国的。   (   )

4. Listening rejoinder. Listen to the dialog and choose the correct response.
   - Ⓐ 新房子和老房子都在纽约。
   - Ⓑ 新房子离老房子很远。
   - Ⓒ 新房子很方便，老房子也很方便。
   - Ⓓ 新房子和老房子的大小、颜色和形状都不一样。   (   )

Speaking

1. Talk about your or a relative's or friend's experiences of moving to a new house.

2. Answer the following questions using 因为… 所以… ; provide two reasons for each question.
   1) What do you want to be in the future? Why?
   2) Where do you want to live in the future? Why?

3. Compare the similarities and differences between the following food in terms of color, shape, and size.
   1) Noodles vs. spaghetti
   2) Ravioli vs. dumplings
   3) Bread vs. a Chinese bun (馒头)

4. Search online about the ancestors of three famous America people and find out where they came from, how they moved to America, and when they moved to America. Then prepare an oral report using the following as an example:

> Barak Obama的爸爸是1959年来美国的。他的爸爸是从肯尼亚(Kěnníyà / Kenya)搬来美国的。

Reading

1. Answer the following questions in Chinese.

   1) 苹果的颜色跟橙子的颜色一样吗？

   2) 篮球的形状跟橄榄球的形状一样吗？

   3) 乒乓球的大小跟足球的大小一样吗？

   4) 中国国旗(guóqí / national flag)的颜色跟美国国旗的颜色一样吗？

   5) 坐飞机跟坐火车一样快吗？

   6) 住在郊区跟住在城市一样方便吗？

   7) 住在家里跟住在学校一样安静吗？

   8) 你今年暑假跟去年暑假过得一样开心吗？

2. Read the paragraph and answer the multiple-choice questions that follow.

马克住在美国西边的一个乡村,十七年前,他出生在这里。小时候,马克喜欢这里安静的生活(shēnghuó life)。后来,他想当律师,要去大城市上大学(dàxué university)。因为东边的好大学很多,所以他觉得高中(gāozhōng high school)毕业(bìyè graduate)以后,他会搬到东边的一个城市去。他不想去纽约,因为纽约太(tài too)大了,很吵,人也很多。他觉得他会(huì will)去波士顿(Bōshìdùn Boston),因为他的爸爸在波士顿出生,他也喜欢海边的城市。

1) 马克从小在哪儿生活?
   Ⓐ 城市　　　　　　　　　Ⓑ 乡村
   Ⓒ 郊区　　　　　　　　　Ⓓ 小区　　　　　　　　(　)

2) 马克为什么喜欢他的家乡(jiāxiāng hometown)?
   Ⓐ 因为那里很安静。
   Ⓑ 因为那里很方便。
   Ⓒ 因为那里有很多好大学。
   Ⓓ 因为他喜欢他的学校。　　　　　　　　(　)

3) 马克为什么想搬到东边?
   Ⓐ 因为他的爸爸的家在波士顿。
   Ⓑ 因为他想去那里上大学。
   Ⓒ 因为他的家要搬到那里。
   Ⓓ 因为他喜欢那里海边的城市。　　　　　　(　)

4) 马克为什么不想去纽约?
   Ⓐ 因为纽约不在海边。
   Ⓑ 因为纽约离他的家太远了。
   Ⓒ 因为纽约太大,太吵,人太多。
   Ⓓ 因为他的爸爸出生在纽约。　　　　　　(　)

3. Guess the riddles.

1) 这个球的形状跟足球一样,颜色跟乒乓球一样,大小跟网球一样。Answer : _____

2) 这个交通工具的形状跟火车一样,颜色跟火车也一样,大小也跟火车一样。火车在地上跑,它在地下跑。Answer : _____

3) 这个地方跟乡村一样安静,它离城市比较近。Answer : _____

4) 这个食物(shíwù / food)的形状跟小船一样,颜色跟馄饨一样,大小也跟馄饨一样。Answer : _____

4. Read the paragraph and determine whether the following statements are true (T) or false (F).

我叫王爱美,是一个美国中学生。我上十年级(niánjí / grade)。我家有五口人,爸爸、妈妈、双胞胎(shuāngbāotāi / twin)妹妹、弟弟和我。我妹妹叫王爱华(huá)。她长得跟我一样。她的头发和眼睛的颜色,还有鼻子、耳朵和嘴巴的大小、形状都跟我一样。所以很多人都分不清(fēn bù qīng / cannot tell)我们。不过,我们也有不一样的地方,比如(bǐrú / such as)爱好。她喜欢运动,我喜欢音乐。她爱安静,我爱热闹(rènao / liveliness)。妹妹和我上同(same)一个学校,同一个年级,但是(dànshì / but)上不同的课。每天早上,妈妈都开车送我们上学,下午再来学校接我们回家。你知道为什么(wèishénme / why)我和妹妹叫爱美和爱华吗?因为我妈妈是中国人,我爸爸是美国人,所以他们给我们取(qǔ / name)爱美和爱华的名字。意思(yìsi / meaning)是爱美国和爱中国。我们都喜欢我们的名字。

1) 王爱美和王爱华都上十年级。( )
2) 王爱美和王爱华的头发、鼻子、眼睛、嘴巴、耳朵都是一样的。( )
3) 王爱美和王爱华的爱好也是一样的。( )
4) 王爱美和妹妹都上一样的课。( )
5) 王爱美的爸爸每天送她们上学,接她们回家。( )
6) "华"的意思是中国。( )

Writing

1. Practice writing the following characters in the correct stroke order.

搬

地方

交通

因为

所 所 所 所 所 所 所 所
以 以 以 以

| 所以 | 所以 | 所以 | | |

跟 跟 跟 跟 跟 跟 跟 跟 跟 跟 跟 跟 跟

| 跟 | 跟 | 跟 | 跟 | | | | |

2. Fill in the blanks with the appropriate vocabulary words.

2010年，＿＿＿＿＿＿＿＿＿＿爸爸的公司(gōngsī company)在北京开了一个分(fēn branch)公司，＿＿＿＿＿＿＿＿＿＿我们一家人也从美国搬到北京。在美国我们住在郊区，很＿＿＿＿＿＿＿＿＿＿，但是不太＿＿＿＿＿＿＿＿＿＿，离很多地方都远。我上学、去同学家都要妈妈开车接、送。在北京我们一开始(kāishǐ beginning)住在城里，离学校很近，离爸爸的公司也很近，很＿＿＿＿＿＿＿＿＿＿。我开心极了。可是(kěshì but)这里离市中心(shìzhōngxīn city center)太近，很＿＿＿＿＿＿＿＿＿＿，路上车很多，人也很多，每天上班下班的时候都＿＿＿＿＿＿＿＿＿＿。后来我们搬到＿＿＿＿＿＿＿＿＿＿。现在我们住的地方很方便，也很安静。我很喜欢。

3. Complete the sentences with a statement that shows a logical outcome, effect, or one that provides a reason for the outcome.

1) 因为城里很吵，_____。

2) 因为郊区很安静，_____。

3) 因为我的家离学校很远，_____。

4) _____，所以我暑假去北京学中文了。

5) _____，所以妈妈会开车接我回家。

4. Write five similarities and five differences between you and your classmates using 一样 and 不一样。

   Example: 我的中文书和我同学的中文书一样新。我和我的同学不一样高。

_____

_____

_____

_____

_____

_____

_____

LESSON 2 MOVING TO A NEW SCHOOL

STEP 3 MAKING COMPARISONS

Listening

1. Listening rejoinder. Listen to the question and choose the correct response.
   - Ⓐ 对，数学课比历史课容易。
   - Ⓑ 对，数学课比历史课难。
   - Ⓒ 不对，数学课比历史课少。
   - Ⓓ 不对，数学课比历史课多。　　　　　　　　　　　　　　　　(　　)

2. Listen to the recording and then the question in English. Choose the correct answer.
   QUESTION: What subject is the person interested in?
   - Ⓐ 音乐和中文
   - Ⓑ 体育和美术
   - Ⓒ 音乐和体育
   - Ⓓ 数学和音乐　　　　　　　　　　　　　　　　　　　　　　(　　)

3. Listen and rank the subjects from the easiest to the hardest according to what you hear.
   - Ⓐ 中文　　　(　　)　　　Ⓑ 数学　　　(　　)
   - Ⓒ 历史　　　(　　)　　　Ⓓ 英文　　　(　　)

4. Listening rejoinder. Listen to the question and choose the correct response.
   - Ⓐ 物理很有意思。
   - Ⓑ 化学课比较多。
   - Ⓒ 你对哪个感兴趣？
   - Ⓓ 物理比化学容易一点。　　　　　　　　　　　　　　　　　(　　)

Speaking

1. What do you think of Chinese food, Indian food, American food, French food, and Japanese food? Provide one sentence for each, using 比较.

2. Answer the following questions.

   1) 你将来想当什么？你现在对哪些科目比较感兴趣？
   2) 你觉得今年哪门课比较难，哪门课比较容易？

3. Work with a partner to compare two American celebrities using five 比 – sentences.

4. Prepare a one-minute speech introducing your family members' professions and their interests, and then share the information with your classmates.

Reading

1. Read the following paragraph and answer the following question in Chinese.

   去年我学过数学、英文、历史、中文和物理。我很喜欢中文和英文，也对数学感兴趣，所以今年还会学这三门课。我觉得历史很无聊，我不是很感兴趣。我也不太喜欢物理，我觉得它比别的课难多了。今年我想读化学和电脑课。

   hui = will
   bié = other

   QUESTION: 今年这个人要学哪五门课？

2. Read the following paragraph and rank the three items in terms of size, function, and convenience from the least to the most.

笔记本电脑、iPad和手机都是很好的电子产品。笔记本电脑最有用。它的功能比iPad和手机大多了。手机最小最轻便，但是功能比笔记本电脑和iPad少得多。iPad比笔记本电脑小，比较轻便。功能比笔记本电脑少，比手机多，是最新的电子产品，很受欢迎。

	笔记本电脑	iPad	手机
size			
function			
convenience			

3. Read the dialog and determine whether the following statements are true (T) or false (F).

A: 你喜欢中国菜还是美国菜？

B: 我都喜欢。

A: 你比较喜欢哪一个？

B: 因为我是美国人，所以我比较喜欢美国菜。

A: 我觉得中国菜比美国菜健康。

B: 美国菜里的肉比中国菜里的肉多多了。

A: 对！西餐里的蔬菜比中餐里的蔬菜少很多。

B: 还有，西餐的甜点也比中餐的甜点多得多。

A: 中餐的味道也比西餐好得多！

B: 我们晚上叫中餐外卖，好吗？

A: 好！

1) 中餐比西餐健康。　　　　　　　　　　（　　）
2) 西餐中的蔬菜比中餐中的少。　　　　　（　　）
3) 中餐中的肉比西餐中的多一点。　　　　（　　）
4) B比较喜欢中餐，因为B是中国人。　　 （　　）
5) 他们晚上要吃中餐。　　　　　　　　　（　　）

Writing

1. Practice writing the following characters in the correct stroke order.

比较

多

少

难

贵

兴 兴 兴 兴 兴 兴
趣 趣 趣 趣 趣 趣 趣 趣 趣 趣 趣 趣 趣 趣

兴趣 | 兴趣 | 兴趣 | |

科 科 科 科 科 科 科 科 科
目 目 目 目 目

科目 | 科目 | 科目 | |

2. Write one sentence expressing your thoughts on the following subjects using 比较 and other adjectives such as 有意思，难，容易，and 无聊.

1) 数学课：_____

2) 化学课：_____

3) 物理课：_____

4) 中文课：_____

5) 生物课：_____

6) 英文课：_____

7) 历史课：_____

3. Write two sentences comparing each pair of modes of transportation listed below. Use the words 快，慢，方便, or 累.

   1) Walking vs. the subway in New York
   2) Walking vs. cycling on a big school campus

   _____

   _____

   _____

4. Write two short paragraphs to compare the following countries. In one paragraph compare the land areas (面积 miànjī), and in the other paragraph compare the populations (人口 rénkǒu).

	China	United States	Canada	United Kingdom	Japan
Land area (sq/km)	9.60 million	9.63 million	9.98 million	244,820	377,835
Population	over 1.3 billion	over 300 million	over 30 million	over 60 million	over 125 million

_____

_____

_____

_____

_____

LESSON 2 MOVING TO A NEW SCHOOL

5. Write an email to your pen pal in China, telling him or her the classes you have this year and compare them to those of last year. Tell your pen pal what you want to do in the future as well as your present interests. Write at least 10 sentences.

LESSON 3 SETTLING INTO A NEW HOME

STEP 1 DESCRIBING THE ROOMS IN A HOUSE

Listening

1. Listen to the description and then the question in English. Choose the correct answer.

   QUESTION: What room is the person talking about?

   A 客厅 　　　　　　　　**B** 餐厅
   C 卧室 　　　　　　　　**D** 卫生间　　　　　　　　　　　（　　）

2. Mark is talking about his house. Check the rooms that are in Mark's house.

   A Kitchen　　　　　　（　　）　　**B** Bedroom　　　　　　（　　）
   C Attic　　　　　　　（　　）　　**D** Study　　　　　　　（　　）
   E Basement　　　　　（　　）　　**F** Dining room　　　　（　　）
   G Living room　　　　（　　）　　**H** Bathroom　　　　　（　　）

3. Fangfang is introducing her new house to her friends. Listen to her description and answer the question in English.

   QUESTION: Where is the master bedroom?

   A On the first floor
   B Next to the dining room
   C On the left side of the hall on the 2nd floor
   D On the right side of the hall on the 2nd floor　　　　　　　　　（　　）

4. Listen to the dialog and determine whether the following statements are true (T) or false (F).

   A Zhang An is downstairs.　　　　　　　　　　　　　　　　　（　　）
   B Zhang An's mother is upstairs.　　　　　　　　　　　　　　（　　）
   C Zhang An's mother is downstairs.　　　　　　　　　　　　　（　　）
   D Zhang An is leaving the house.　　　　　　　　　　　　　　（　　）

Speaking

1. Imagine that you spent last Saturday at home. Talk about your activities during the day; be sure to mention the time and location for each activity.

2. You are going to a sleep over at your friend's house. How would you ask the location of the rooms that you will probably be in (bedroom, bathroom, kitchen, living room/family room)? Create at least three questions.

3. Study the floor plan and tell on which floor the following rooms are located: kitchen, master bedroom, living room, and study.

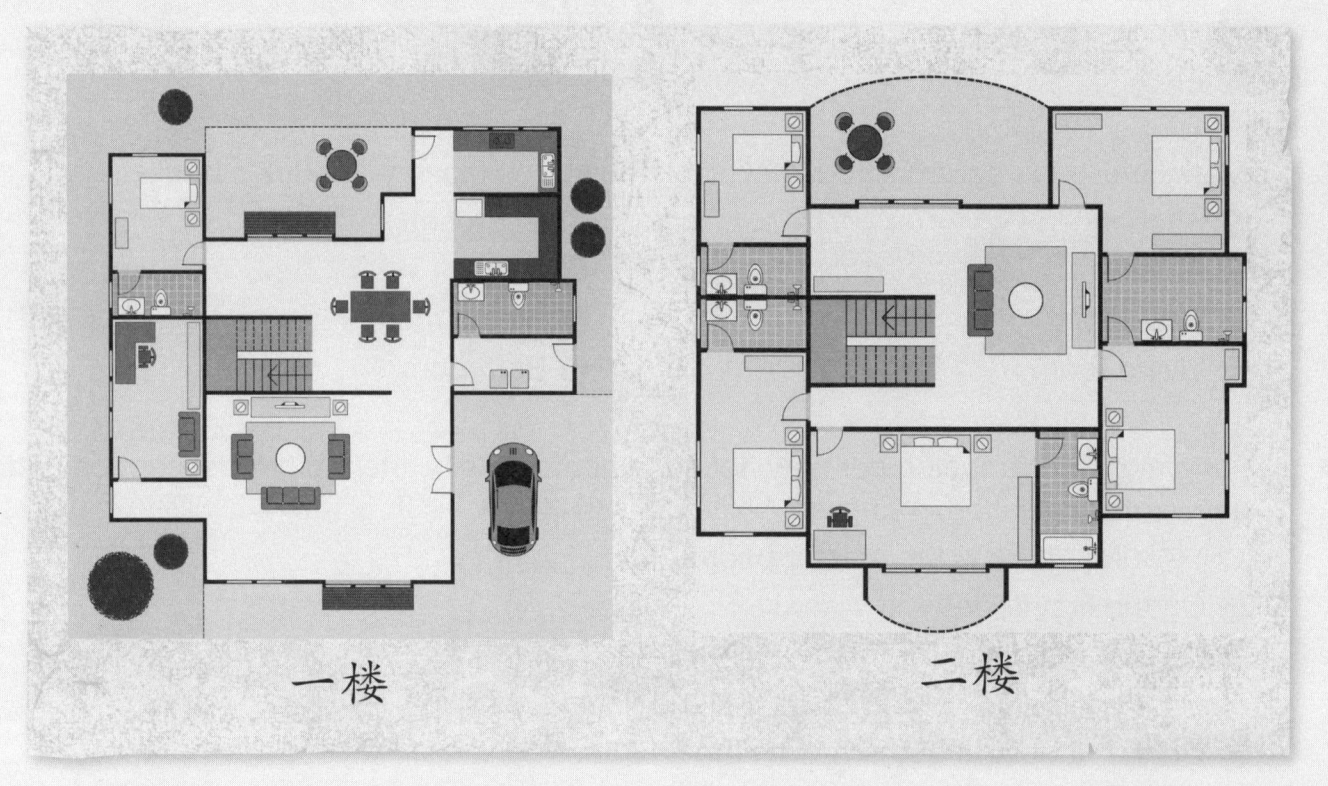

一楼　　　　　二楼

4. Design the interior of a one-story house for a family of four: father, mother, son (a high school senior), and daughter (a middle school student). Draw a simple floor plan and tell a classmate where the rooms are located.

Reading

1. Match the descriptions on the left with the correct rooms on the right.

   1) 最大的睡房　　　　　　　A) 地下室
   2) 洗手、洗澡的房间　　　　B) 厨房
   3) 做饭的地方　　　　　　　C) 主卧室
   4) 房子里最高的房间　　　　D) 卫生间
   5) 房子里最低的房间　　　　E) 阁楼

2. Look at the diagrams and the accompanying statements. Select the correct word from the options below to describe each statement.

   Ⓐ 请进来　　　Ⓑ 请出去　　　Ⓒ 请进去　　　Ⓓ 请出来
   Ⓔ 请下来　　　Ⓕ 请上去　　　Ⓖ 请下去　　　Ⓗ 请上来

   1) 芳芳 asks 安琪 to come in.　　　(　)
   2) 安琪 asks 芳芳 to come out.　　　(　) 
   3) 芳芳 asks 安琪 to go out.　　　(　) 
   4) 芳芳 asks 安琪 to go in.　　　(　) 
   5) 芳芳 asks 安琪 to come up.　　　(　) 
   6) 安琪 asks 芳芳 to come down.　　　(　) 
   7) 芳芳 asks 安琪 to go up.　　　(　) 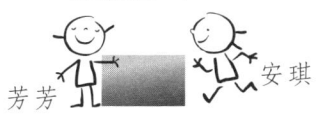
   8) 芳芳 asks 安琪 to go down.　　　(　) 

LESSON 3 MOVING TO A NEW SCHOOL

3. Based on the picture, determine whether the following descriptions are true (T) or false (F).

1) 这是客厅。 (　　)
2) 窗户上挂着窗帘。 (　　)
3) 地上摆着一张沙发。 (　　)
4) 沙发的前边放着一张咖啡桌。 (　　)
5) 墙上挂着三幅画。 (　　)
6) 墙边的桌子上放着一盏台灯。 (　　)

4. Read the following paragraph on Ding Qiang's house and answer the questions in Chinese.

> 我家一进门是门厅，这里放着两把椅子。门厅的右边是客厅。客厅里有沙发和咖啡桌。我和家人周末喜欢在这里看电视。客厅的对面是厨房，客厅和厨房的中间是走廊。走廊的左边是主卧室和卫生间，右边是我的房间。

1) 门厅里有什么？

_____

2) 客厅在哪里？

_____

3) 丁强和家人周末喜欢做什么？

_____

4) 走廊的左边是什么？右边是什么？

_____

Writing

1. Practice writing the following characters in the correct stroke order.

朝 朝 朝 朝 朝 朝 朝 朝 朝 朝 朝 朝

朝

卧 卧 卧 卧 卧 卧 卧 卧
室 室 室 室 室 室 室 室 室

卧室

阳 阳 阳 阳 阳 阳
台 台 台 台 台

阳台

进 进 进 进 进 进 进

进

出 出 出 出 出

出

请 请请请请请请请请请请

沙 沙沙沙沙沙沙沙
发 发发发发发

沙发 沙发 沙发

2. List the rooms in your house.

_____

_____

3. List the furniture you would like to have in your living room and bedroom.

Living room:

_____

_____

Bedroom:

_____

_____

4. Create at least five sentences describing to whom a room or an item in your house belongs.

   Example: 书房里的书架是爸爸的。

   _____

   _____

   _____

   _____

   _____

5. Draw a floor map(s) of your home, label each room, and write a description of the home. Be sure to talk about the locations of each room.

   _____

   _____

   _____

LESSON 3 MOVING TO A NEW SCHOOL

STEP 2 ARRANGING FURNITURE

Listening

1. Listen to the description and then the question in English. Choose the correct answer.

   QUESTION: Which one of the following rooms contains the items mentioned?

   Ⓐ 客厅　　　　　　　　　　　Ⓑ 饭厅

   Ⓒ 厨房　　　　　　　　　　　Ⓓ 书房　　　　　　　　　(　　)

2. Listening rejoinder. Listen to the information and choose the most appropriate response that follows the statements.

   Ⓐ 她是一个医生。　　　　　　Ⓑ 她的房子很大。

   Ⓒ 她很喜欢花。　　　　　　　Ⓓ 她的电脑不在书房。　　(　　)

3. Listen to the dialog and choose the correct statement that explains what is happening.

   Ⓐ Her room is big.　　　　　　Ⓑ Her room is a study room.

   Ⓒ She likes her lamp.　　　　　Ⓓ They are arranging the furniture.　(　　)

4. Listen to how Mike wants to arrange his furniture, and determine whether the following statements are true (T) or false (F).

   Ⓐ He wants to put his bed in front of the window.　　　　　　　(　　)

   Ⓑ He wants to put a table next to the bed.　　　　　　　　　　(　　)

   Ⓒ He wants to put his computer and bag on the floor.　　　　　(　　)

   Ⓓ He wants to put a map and some pictures on the wall.　　　　(　　)

Speaking

1. Talk about the appliances that you have in your home. Also think of one appliance that you do not have but would like to see in your home. If there are no appliances that you would like, then imagine a new appliance that will be invented in the future, give it a name, and tell what it will be used for. Be sure to use the correct measure words when talking about the appliances.

2. Mike is helping his Chinese host family move into a new house. Talk about where he should put the following items:
   1) bike
   2) vase
   3) carpet
   4) sofa
   5) microwave oven
   6) lamp
   7) coffee table

3. Imagine and describe the living room of Mr. Brown's home. He loves to read and has many books in his home. Create at least five sentences using 着.

4. Xiao Li is preparing a bedroom for a visitor. The visitor loves reading books. She also likes art and painting. Paintings with flowers are her favorite works of art. She also needs to have dark curtains and a carpet in her room. What will Xiao Li do? Create at least five sentences using 把.

Reading

1. Put the following words into the rooms or places where they most likely would be found. Some items may be found in more than one room.

> 书架，台灯，洗衣机，烘干机，冰箱，洗碗机，沙发，咖啡桌，电视柜，床，衣柜，自行车，微波炉，花瓶，浴缸，马桶

1) 卧室：_____

2) 厨房：_____

3) 客厅：_____

4) 卫生间：_____

5) 车库：_____

6) 书房：_____

7) 地下室：_____

2. Match the descriptions on the left with the correct words on the right.

1) 这里挂着很多衣服。   A) 冰箱
2) 这里放着很多书。   B) 美术馆
3) 这里种着很多花。   C) 花园
4) 这里挂着很多画。   D) 书房
5) 这里放着很多吃的。   E) 衣柜

3. Your family has just moved into a new house. You need to help with arranging items in the living room. Read the instructions and put the furniture in the right place by putting the corresponding letters in the correct places.

请把大沙发放到窗前，把咖啡桌放到沙发前。把地毯
pū
铺在地中间，把落地灯放在沙发的左边。把两幅画挂在左
lay
边的墙上，把钟挂在右边的墙上。最后，请把绿色植物放
qiángjiǎo
在窗户右边的墙角。
corner

A 沙发   B 咖啡桌   C 地毯   D 落地灯
E 两幅画   F 钟   G 植物

窗户

墙   墙

Floor plan of living room

4. Read the following paragraph and answer the questions in Chinese.

这是小明家的客厅。客厅很大，地上铺着黑白色的地毯，墙上挂着很多幅美丽(měilì)的中国画。客厅中间摆着一张红色的沙发。沙发的前边放着一张棕色的咖啡桌。桌上摆着一个绿色的花瓶，里面插着五颜六色(wǔ yán liù sè)的鲜花(xiānhuā)。客厅的窗户很大，上边挂着银色的窗帘。窗户边摆着一个书柜，里面放着很多书。书柜的旁边还摆着一把黄色的椅子。小明很喜欢他家的客厅。他常常(chángcháng)在这里看电视，和朋友聊天。

1) 小明家的客厅里有什么家具？

_____

2) 小明家有电视吗？

_____

3) 客厅里的沙发是什么颜色的？

_____

4) 沙发的前边有什么？

_____

5) 小明常常在客厅里做什么？

_____

LESSON 3 MOVING TO A NEW SCHOOL

Writing

1. Practice writing the following characters in the correct stroke order.

树 树树树树树树树树树

花 花花花花花花花

着 着着着着着着着着着

种 种种种种种种种种

放 放放放放放放放

挂 挂挂挂挂挂挂挂挂

插 插插插插插插插插插插

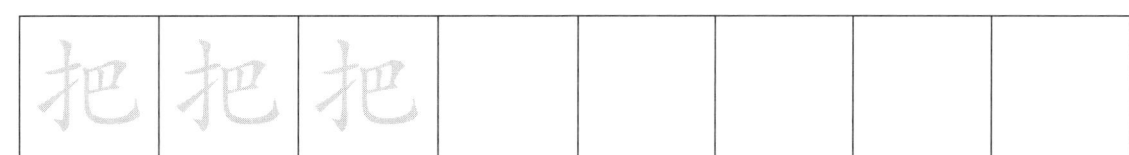

摆 摆摆摆摆摆摆摆摆摆摆摆摆摆
摆 | 摆 | 摆 | 摆 | | | | |

把把把把把把把
把 | 把 | 把 | 把 | | | | |

2. List five appliances you have in your home.

_____

_____

3. Fill in the blanks with the appropriate measure words.

1) 两 (　　) 镜子　　　　4) 一 (　　) 地毯

2) 两 (　　) 台灯　　　　5) 一 (　　) 电冰箱

3) 两 (　　) 床　　　　　6) 三 (　　) 中国画

4. Imagine that you have just moved into your dream house. Describe the furniture in each of the following locations using 着.

客厅里：

1) _____

2) _____

卧室里：

1) _____

2) _____

LESSON 3 MOVING TO A NEW SCHOOL

厨房里：

1) _____

2) _____

车库里：

1) _____

2) _____

5. This room is a bit messy. How do you want to tidy it up? Write at least four sentences using the 把 structure to explain where you would place certain items or what you would change.

Example: 我要把椅子放在桌子前边。

_____

_____

_____

_____

STEP 3 LISTING AND DESCRIBING OBJECTS

Listening

1. Listen and choose the item that belongs to the same category.
   - **A** 火腿
   - **B** 米饭
   - **C** 比萨
   - **D** 可乐   (   )

2. Listen to the sentences and choose the item that was not mentioned.
   - **A** 衣柜
   - **B** 书架
   - **C** 咖啡桌
   - **D** 椅子   (   )

3. Listening rejoinder. Listen to the question and choose the most appropriate response to the question.
   - **A** 我喜欢喝咖啡。
   - **B** 我有一张圆形的咖啡桌。
   - **C** 我喜欢长方形的。
   - **D** 我的客厅里有一个咖啡桌。   (   )

4. Listening rejoinder. Choose the most appropriate response to the question.
   - **A** 我的电脑是苹果的。
   - **B** 我的电脑是方的。
   - **C** 我的电脑是深灰色的。
   - **D** 我的电脑在桌子上。   (   )

Speaking

1. What are the appliances in your household? List them using 像…什么的.

2. Do you like fruits? State the fruits you like using 如…等.

3. Talk about the furniture in your room. Be sure to mention the color of each item of furniture.

4. Describe the color of the clothes that one of your classmates is wearing today.

Reading

1. Match the item on the left with the correct category on the right.

   1) 洗衣机　　　　　　　　A) 文具
   2) 铅笔　　　　　　　　　B) 家具
   3) 沙发　　　　　　　　　C) 水果
   4) 西瓜　　　　　　　　　D) 花
   5) 茉莉　　　　　　　　　E) 蔬菜
   6) 黄瓜　　　　　　　　　F) 中餐
   7) 炒饭　　　　　　　　　G) 电器
   8) 面包　　　　　　　　　H) 西餐

2. Match the national flags of the four countries to the right colors each of them has.

   　　　　　　　　　　　　A) 红色
   　　　　　　　　　　　　B) 粉红色
   1) 中国　　　　　　　　　C) 棕色
   2) 美国　　　　　　　　　D) 白色
   3) 印度　　　　　　　　　E) 黑色
   4) 巴西　　　　　　　　　F) 黄色
   　　　　　　　　　　　　G) 灰色
   　　　　　　　　　　　　H) 绿色
   　　　　　　　　　　　　I) 蓝色

3. Solve the riddles below and write the correct answer in Chinese.

   1) 它是长方形的，打开以后，有两个长方形，下边的长方形上还有很多按键，有的按键是正方形的，有的按键是长方形的。很多人都有，人们用它打字、写电子邮件、上网等。

   ànjiàn　　　　　　　　　　　　　　　　　　　　　　　　
   按键 key　　yòng　dǎzì
   　　　　　　用　　打字
   　　　　　　use　　type

   Answer : _____

2) 它是正方形的，常常是红色或者是金黄色的。上面常常写着黑色的"福"字。在中国新年的时候，人们常常把它贴在门上和墙上。

Answer : _____

4. Read the following paragraph and choose the most appropriate answer to the questions.

> 我家在美国东边的一个小镇。这里离纽约不远，但是很安静，很美丽。我家的房子朝南，有上下两楼。楼下有厨房、餐厅、客厅、一个卧室和一个书房。楼上是爸爸妈妈的卧室，还有我的卧室和弟弟的卧室。我们的房子是浅黄色的，不是很大，但是很漂亮。房子的前边是一个小花园。花园是椭圆形的，里边种着茉莉、水仙和丁香。花园东边是一个浅蓝色的小房子，我们把桌子和椅子放在那里。春天的时候，我们会把它们搬出来，在院子里坐一坐，聊聊天。我很喜欢我的家。

1. 我家的花园在哪儿？
    A 纽约 B 小镇里
    C 我家房子的前边 D 我家房子的后边 (　)

2. 我家的花园里没有什么花？
    A 水仙 B 茉莉
    C 菊花 D 丁香 (　)

3. 花园东边的小房子里放着什么？
   Ⓐ 桌子　　　　　　　　　Ⓑ 椅子
   Ⓒ 冰箱　　　　　　　　　Ⓓ 桌子和椅子　　　　　　（　）

4. 我家的房子是什么颜色的？
   Ⓐ 深红色　　　　　　　　Ⓑ 浅绿色
   Ⓒ 浅黄色　　　　　　　　Ⓓ 浅绿色　　　　　　　　（　）

5. 花园是什么形状的？
   Ⓐ 圆形　　　　　　　　　Ⓑ 长方形
   Ⓒ 椭圆形　　　　　　　　Ⓓ 三角形　　　　　　　　（　）

Writing

1. Practice writing the following characters in the correct stroke order.

像 像像像像像像像像像像

例如 例例例例例例例例
如如如如如如

正方形 正正正正正
方方方方
形形形形形形形

三角形

2. Describe the shapes of the following:

   1) The US President's office : _____

   2) Pentagon : _____

   3) Eggs : _____

   4) Yield sign : _____

   5) A basketball : _____

   6) An American football : _____

3. Complete the sentences.

   1) 厨房里有一些电器，

   _____

   2) 客厅里有很多家具，

   _____

   3) 他喜欢吃水果，

   _____

4) 她妹妹的宠物很多，

_____

5) 她的书包里有很多文具，

_____

6) 她爸爸去过很多国家，

_____

4. Write a paragraph describing your room, including the furniture, decorations, etc. Be sure to talk about the colors and shapes of the items. Start with the location of your room. Write at least 10 sentences.

_____

_____

_____

_____

_____

_____

_____

_____

LESSON 4 — ADAPTING TO THE WEATHER

STEP 1 TALKING ABOUT THE WEATHER

Listening

1. Listen to the weather forecast and decide which activity would be best to do because of the forecast.
   - **A** Go jogging tonight.
   - **B** Go cycling in the afternoon.
   - **C** Go for a picnic this morning.
   - **D** Go to the beach this afternoon.   (   )

2. Listening rejoinder. Listen to the question and choose the correct response.
   - **A** 明天我要去海边。
   - **B** 明天没有雨，是晴天。
   - **C** 他喜欢冷的天气。
   - **D** 我今天不会去公园。   (   )

3. Listen to the dialog and then the question in English. Choose the correct answer.
   QUESTION: Why does Mark want to stay home tomorrow?
   - **A** The weather has been good these days.
   - **B** It will be much colder tomorrow.
   - **C** It will be a nice day tomorrow.
   - **D** The weather is good today.   (   )

4. Listen to the weather forecast and describe each segment of the day using corresponding letters that represent the weather symbols.

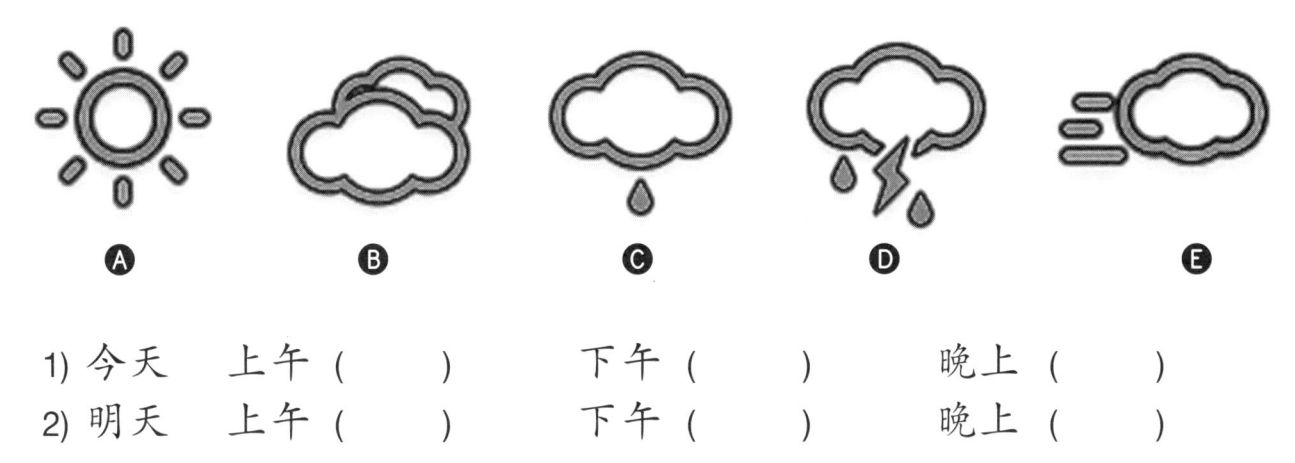

   A   **B**   **C**   **D**   **E**

   1) 今天   上午 (   )   下午 (   )   晚上 (   )
   2) 明天   上午 (   )   下午 (   )   晚上 (   )

Speaking

1. Read the weekly weather forecast below and tell your friend the weather for the next two days.

星期一	星期二	星期三	星期四	星期五	星期六	星期天
☀	☁	🌧	⛈	☀	☁	🌬☁
60-75°F	55-70°F	50-70°F	48-65°F	63-78°F	58-68°F	53-68°F
15.5-23.8°C	12.7-21.1°C	10-21.1°C	8.8-18.3°C	17.2-25.5°C	14.4-20°C	11.6-20°C

2. Based on the same weather forecast in Question 1, ask and answer questions on the temperatures this weekend.

3. Compare the weather below for Saturday and Sunday, and tell which day you think is a good day for a Frisbee game.

   Saturday: Sunny 40°F to 50°F wind 10 to 12m/h
   Sunday: Cloudy 35°F to 40°F   wind 0 to 5m/h

Reading

1. Read the following cell phone text from your friend and choose what would be the best plan for tomorrow according to your friend's suggestion.

   "明天天气很不好，下雨又有大风，我们不去爬山了。你要过来一起看电影吗？"

   Ⓐ 爬山   Ⓑ 看电影
   Ⓒ 放风筝   Ⓓ 踢足球   (   )

2. Read the weather chart and find a day for each of the following activities.

3月27日（星期三）	晴	低温9°C ~ 高温16°C	东南风 1 ~ 2 级 jí level
3月28日（星期四）	多云	低温9°C ~ 高温18°C	没有风
3月29日（星期五）	雨	低温8°C ~ 高温13°C	南风 5 级
3月30日（星期六）	晴	低温11°C ~ 高温16°C	东南风 3 ~ 4 级

1) Hiking: _____

2) Flying a kite: _____

3) Reading at home: _____

4) Cycling: _____

3. Read the paragraph and determine whether the following statements are true (T) or false (F).

今天是四月二十日，星期六。上海这个周末的天气很好！今天白天晴，气温十五到二十度，没有风。晚上阴，有小雨，气温十到十四度。明天上午多云，下午晴，气温十六到二十二度，东南风1-2级。下个星期的气温比这个星期的气温高。最高温是二十五度，最低温是十六度。

Ⓐ 这个周末上海的天气不好。 (　　)
Ⓑ 上海星期六是晴天，星期日下雨。 (　　)
Ⓒ 星期六的气温比星期日的高很多。 (　　)
Ⓓ 下个星期的气温比这个星期的气温高一点。 (　　)

Writing

1. Practice writing the following characters in the correct stroke order.

晴 晴晴晴晴晴晴晴晴晴晴晴晴

阴 阴阴阴阴阴阴

风 风风风风

雨 雨雨雨雨雨雨雨雨

雷 雷雷雷雷雷雷雷雷雷雷雷雷

冷 冷冷冷冷冷冷冷

热 热热热热热热热热热热

气 气 气 气
温 温 温 温 温 温 温 温 温 温 温

气温 | 气温 | 气温 | | |

度 度 度 度 度 度 度 度 度

度 | 度 | 度 | | | | |

低 低 低 低 低 低 低

低 | 低 | 低 | | | | |

2. Describe the weather according to the symbols.

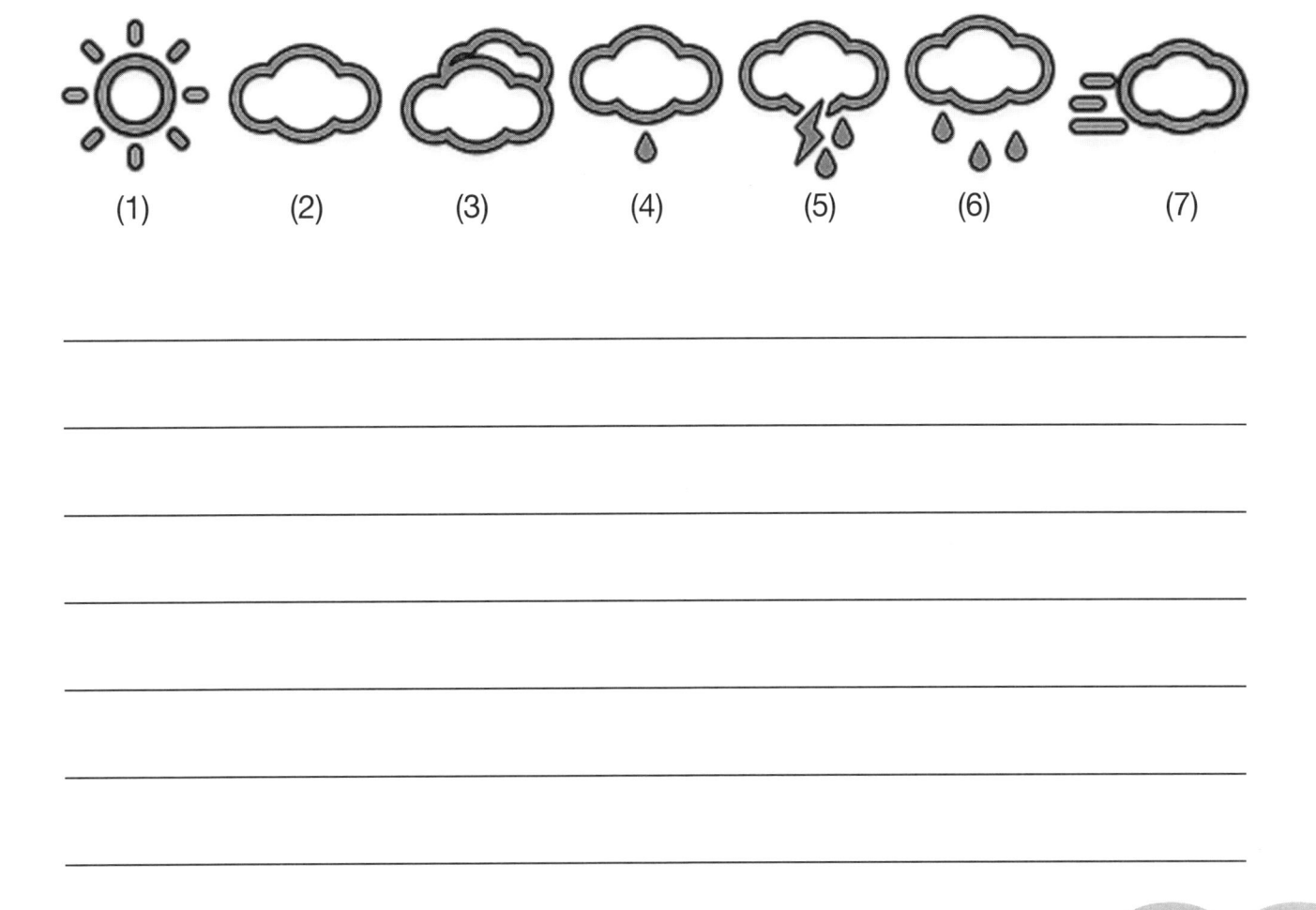

(1)　　(2)　　(3)　　(4)　　(5)　　(6)　　(7)

_____

_____

_____

_____

_____

_____

LESSON 4 ADAPTING TO THE WEATHER

3. Find out the weather in your area for the coming week and complete the following weather forecast.

日期							
天气							
气温							

4. Compare the monthly temperatures of the four cities using any of these patterns:
   A + 比 + B + adjective + 多了
   A + 比 + B + adjective + 一点
   A + 和 + B + 一样 + adjective

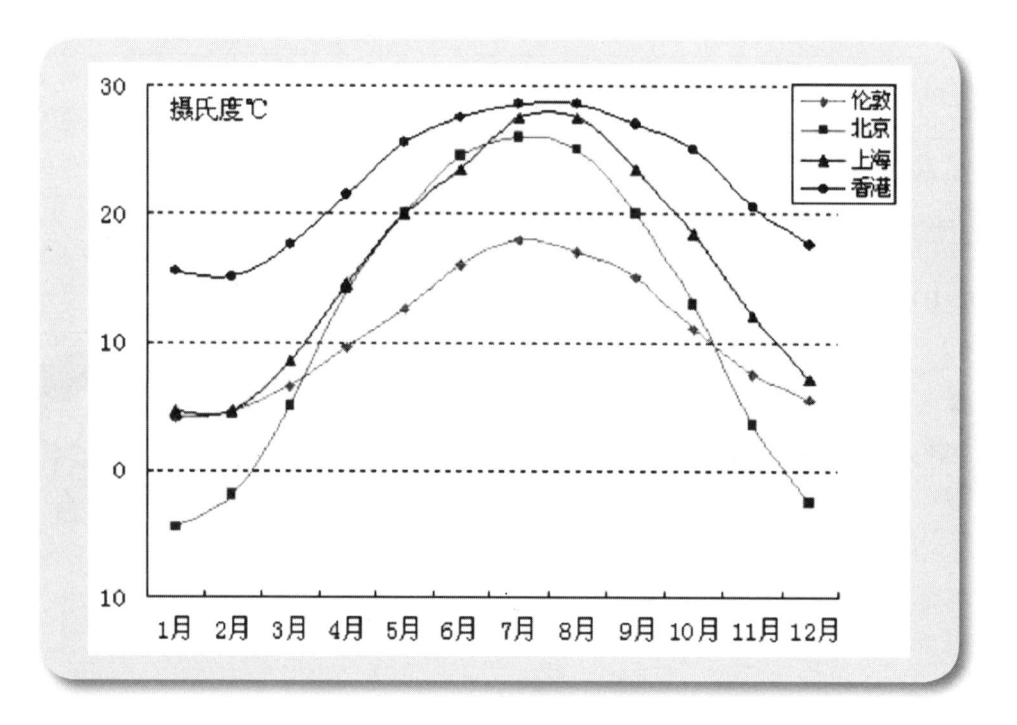

Example: 一月　　　北京 vs 香港

北京的气温比香港的气温低多了。

1) 一月　　　上海 vs 伦敦

_____

2) 一月　　　北京 vs 伦敦

_____

3) 四月　　　香港 vs 上海

_____

4) 五月　　　北京 vs 上海
   _____

5) 七月　　　伦敦 vs 香港
   _____

6) 七月　　　上海 vs 香港
   _____

7) 九月　　　伦敦 vs 北京
   _____

8) 十月　　　北京 vs 香港
   _____

9) 十二月　　伦敦 vs 上海
   _____

10) 十二月　　香港 vs 北京
    _____

5. Choose a city from the list below. Check its weather today and tomorrow. Then write a paragraph describing the weather there and compare it with your local weather. Write at least 10 sentences.

> 北京，上海，香港，西安，纽约，洛杉矶 (LA)，
> 迈阿密 (Miami)，悉尼 (Sydney)，伦敦

_____

_____

_____

_____

LESSON 4 ADAPTING TO THE WEATHER

STEP 2 DRESSING ACCORDING TO THE WEATHER

Listening

1. Listen to a set of clothing items. Cross out the item from the list below when you hear it. Of the remaining items, which one will you wear to the beach?

    A 毛衣　　　**B** 领带　　　**C** 短裤　　　**D** 衬衫
    E 高跟鞋　　**F** 帽子　　　**G** 围巾　　　**H** 太阳镜　　　(　　)

2. Listen to the statement and decide what the weather probably is.

    A Cloudy, 65°F to 75°F, wind 10m/h　　**B** Rain, 70°F to 75°F, wind 5m/h
    C Snow, 50°F to 60°F　　　　　　　　　**D** Sunny, 75°F to 85°F, wind 5-10m/h　(　　)

3. Listen to the statement and choose the most appropriate response.
    A You need to wear a raincoat and sneakers.
    B You need to wear a sweater and a jacket to stay warm.
    C You need to wear shorts and slippers because it is hot.
    D You need to wear sunglasses and bring an umbrella.　　　　(　　)

4. Listen and decide where the person is most likely going.
    A She is going to the beach.
    B She is going skiing.
    C She is going to visit a friend in Florida.
    D She is going to play tennis.　　　　(　　)

Speaking

1. Imagine a friend is moving to one of the following places: Hawaii or Alaska. Work in pairs and make a list of clothes your friend needs to buy for each of the two places.

2. Read the weather forecast below and tell your (imaginary) younger brother what to put on for a beach day using appropriate verbs and measure words.

    今天：晴。气温：75 到 90 华氏度。没有风。

3. Imagine that you are going to attend your sister's high school graduation ceremony at the end of May. The ceremony will be held outdoors in the football stadium. You are hoping that it will be a nice day. Describe what you need to wear that day. Use appropriate verbs and measure words.

4. Talk about the clothes you plan to wear every day of the week from Monday to Friday and explain why by describing the predicted weather.

Reading

1. Match the measures words with the appropriate clothing items.

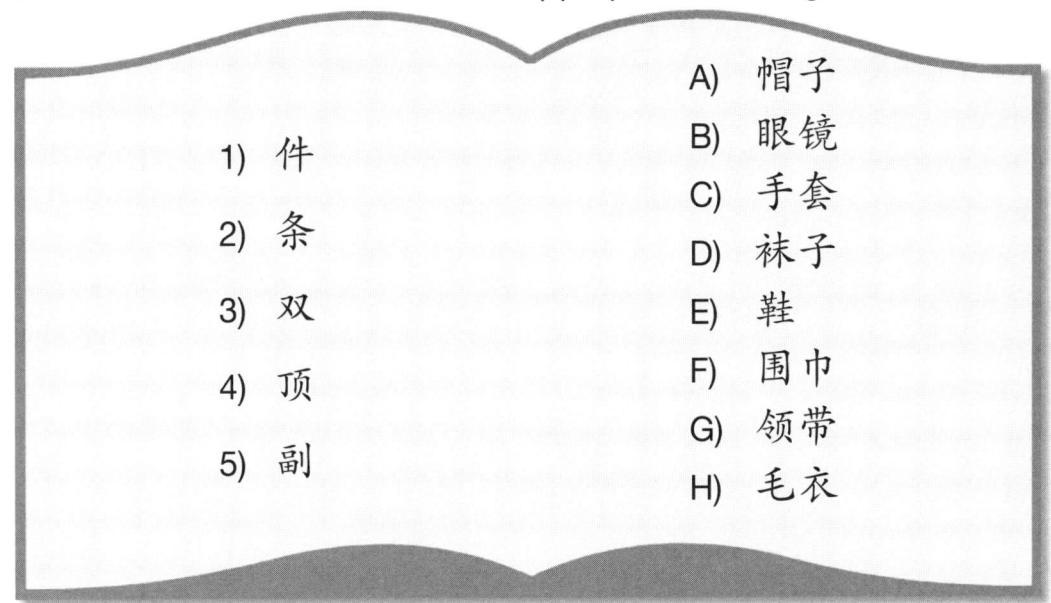

   1) 件
   2) 条
   3) 双
   4) 顶
   5) 副

   A) 帽子
   B) 眼镜
   C) 手套
   D) 袜子
   E) 鞋
   F) 围巾
   G) 领带
   H) 毛衣

2. Match the clothing with the appropriate occasion.

   1) 衬衫，领带，皮鞋
   2) 连衣裙，高跟鞋
   3) 牛仔裤，T恤衫，凉鞋
   4) 运动服，运动鞋

   A) 打篮球
   B) 毕业舞会 (bìyè wǔhuì) prom
   C) 上班
   D) 和朋友看电影

3. Read the paragraph about the contents of a wardrobe and tell where the person most probably lives.

这是我的衣柜。衣柜里有很多T恤衫、短裤和泳衣，还有很多双凉鞋。我还有很多太阳镜和帽子。衣柜里没有羽绒服，也没有手套和围巾。

A Chicago ( )
B Boston ( )
C Honolulu ( )
D New York ( )

4. Read the paragraph and answer the following questions.

中国北京一年有四季，每个季节的天气都不同。春天是3月到5月，天气暖和，但是多风，有时候也会有低气温，所以三月的时候人们还是得穿比较厚的衣服，如毛衣、风衣，还戴帽子、围巾。夏天很热，人们周末会穿短衣、短裤和凉鞋。秋天很凉爽，人们会穿衬衫、T恤衫和长裤。但是有时候也会有高温天气，人们叫它"秋老虎"。这个时候你得穿得少一点。北京的冬天很冷，人们常穿羽绒服和靴子，还会戴帽子、围巾。

dànshì – but
huì – will
hòu – thick
windbreaker
liángshuǎng – cooling

1) 北京春天的天气怎么样？

_____

2) 夏天去北京，得穿什么衣服？

_____

3) 北京人在冬天常穿什么衣服？

_____

4) 什么是秋老虎？

_____

Writing

1. Practice writing the following characters in the correct stroke order.

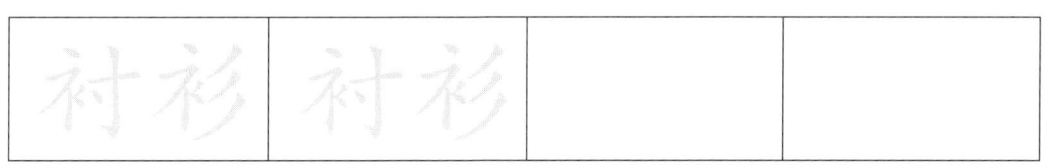

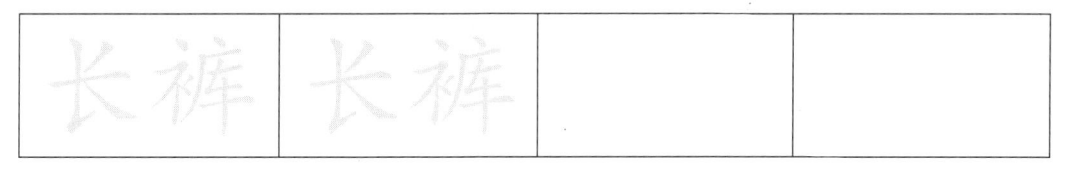

衬衫

长裤

短裙

球鞋

手套

2. Write down what outdoor clothing you wear during the following seasons where you live.

春天：_____

夏天：_____

秋天：_____

冬天：_____

3. What clothing do you normally wear to a formal concert? (Answer in full sentences in Chinese.)

_____
_____
_____
_____

4. In fall, what do you wear for school on weekdays and what do you wear on weekends? (Answer in full sentences in Chinese.)

_____
_____
_____
_____

5. Compare the weather in New York and Hawaii on New Year's Day, and then compare how people from both places are dressed on January 1st.

_____

_____

_____

_____

_____

_____

STEP 3 DESCRIBING HOW PEOPLE ARE DRESSED

Listening

1. Listen to the description and decide which person it is.

   ( )

2. Listening rejoinder. Listen to the question and choose the most appropriate response.
   - Ⓐ 我妹妹今年九岁。
   - Ⓑ 我妹妹喜欢红色。
   - Ⓒ 穿红色短裙的女孩是我妹妹。
   - Ⓓ 我喜欢妹妹的红裙子。

   ( )

3. Mark's older brother and sister are in the photo below. Listen to Mark's description and identify them.

   明明
   小东
   芳芳
   玛丽

   Mark's older brother: _____

   Mark's older sister: _____

4. Listen to the description and select the correct statement that explains what you hear.

   Ⓐ It is winter; people are staying in a hotel.

   Ⓑ It is summer; people are at the beach.

   Ⓒ People are traveling.

   Ⓓ People are in an indoor swimming pool.   (   )

Speaking

1. Describe what you are wearing today. Use the appropriate verb, 着, and measure words.

2. Find a family picture and work with a partner to identify each person in the picture by asking and answering questions. Ask questions describing the person's attire. For example, 穿牛仔裤的男生是谁？是你弟弟吗？

3. People wear different clothing for different occasions. Here are three occasions or locales: a birthday party, a beach, and a graduation ceremony. With a partner, describe the kind of clothing people would be wearing for that occasion or place and have your partner guess where the people are.

Reading

1. Read the paragraph and match the clothing with the person.

   我爸爸是一个公司(gōngsī)的经理(jīnglǐ)。我妈妈是大学(dàxué)的老师。我哥哥是高中(gāozhōng)的足球运动员。我是小学生，我喜欢户外活动(hùwài huódòng)。

   1) 连衣裙、高跟鞋   A) 我

   2) 短裤、球鞋   B) 妈妈

   3) 衬衫、长裤和领带   C) 哥哥

   4) 太阳镜、T恤衫、短裙   D) 爸爸

2. Read the paragraph and select the picture that fits the description.

> 爸爸、弟弟和我都穿着短裤,妈妈和弟弟都穿着衬衫,爸爸穿着T恤衫。

( )

3. Read the paragraph and answer the questions.

> Mr. Smith 是我的校长,他常常(chángcháng)穿着深色的大衣和长裤,里面是白色的衬衫,还戴着领带。他喜欢打篮球,所以他有时候也穿篮球运动服和球鞋。
>
> often

1. Mr. Smith 常常穿什么?
   _____

2. Mr. Smith 在篮球场上常常穿什么?
   Ⓐ 大衣、衬衫和领带　　　Ⓑ 运动服和球鞋　　　( )

Writing

1. Practice writing the following characters in the correct stroke order.

着

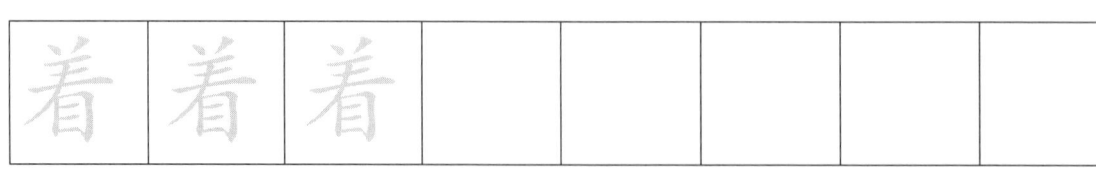

戴

2. Fill in the blanks with the appropriate words.

1) 他头上（　　　　）一顶红色的（　　　　）。

2) 他手上（　　　　）一双白色的（　　　　）。

3) 他身上（　　　　）一件绿色的衬衫。

4) 他脚上（　　　　）一双蓝色的（　　　　）。

5) 他还（　　　　）一副黑色的太阳镜。

3. Describe how each person in the picture is dressed using 着.

1) 她 _____。

2) 他 _____。

4. Find a family picture; write a paragraph of at least five sentences introducing each person. Follow this sentence pattern: 穿红色上衣、黑色长裤的是我的爸爸。

_____

_____

_____

_____

_____

_____

LESSON 5 DISCOVERING THE COMMUNITY

STEP 1 FINDING PLACES IN THE COMMUNITY

Listening

1. Check the facilities you hear in the statement.
   - Ⓐ 便利店　　　　（　　）
   - Ⓑ 医院　　　　　（　　）
   - Ⓒ 洗衣店　　　　（　　）
   - Ⓓ 理发店　　　　（　　）
   - Ⓔ 公园　　　　　（　　）
   - Ⓕ 警察局　　　　（　　）
   - Ⓖ 银行　　　　　（　　）

2. Listen to the short dialog and answer the question.
   QUESTION: Where are the hairdressers' salons located?
   - Ⓐ 西北边和东北边
   - Ⓑ 东南边和西南边
   - Ⓒ 西北边和西南边
   - Ⓓ 西南边和东北边　　　　（　　）

3. Listening rejoinder. Listen to the question and choose the most appropriate response.
   - Ⓐ 这个社区人很多。
   - Ⓑ 这个社区不大，也不小。
   - Ⓒ 这个社区是我最喜欢的。
   - Ⓓ 这个社区不但有便利店、超市和医院，而且还有银行和邮局，方便极了。　　　　（　　）

4. Listen to the dialog and answer the question.
   QUESTION: Where does the conversation most likely take place?
   - Ⓐ 银行
   - Ⓑ 餐馆
   - Ⓒ 书店
   - Ⓓ 诊所　　　　（　　）

Speaking

1. Make a 1-minute recording introducing the places in your community, and ask questions on the same topic to your audience.

2. Draw a map of your community showing at least five places; prepare a description of the locations of these places for the next day's class.

3. Do you like the community where your school is located? Give three reasons why you think it is or is not a convenient community using 不但…而且….

Reading

1. Match the following directions in English with the right ones in Chinese.

   1) Northwest   A) 东北
   2) Northeast   B) 东南
   3) Southwest   C) 西北
   4) Southeast   D) 西南

2. Study the map below and determine whether the following statements are true (T) or false (F).

   图书馆   商场   电影院
   停车场   西餐厅   停车场
             公园
   中餐馆   便利店   银行
         zhùzháiqū
         住宅区
         residential area
       邮局
             医院   北

   1) 邮局在社区的东南边。   (   )
   2) 公园在住宅区的北边。   (   )
   3) 停车场在社区的东北边。   (   )
   4) 医院在社区的西南边。   (   )

5) 图书馆的南边有一个餐馆。　　（　　　）
6) 便利店离住宅区很近。　　　　（　　　）
7) 电影院离邮局很远。　　　　　（　　　）

3. Fill in the blanks based on the map in Question 2.

1) 在这个社区吃饭很方便，这里不但有(　　　　　)，而且还有(　　　　　)。

2) 这个社区的东北边很热闹(rènao/lively)，不但有(　　　　　)，而且还有(　　　　　)。

3) 住在这里很方便，住宅区不但离(　　　　　)很近，而且离(　　　　　)也很近。

4) 在这个社区停车很方便，社区的(　　　　　)有停车场，(　　　　　)也有停车场。

4. Read the paragraph and answer the following questions.

我家在美国的东北部(bù/area)。社区很小，但是(dànshì/but)很方便，因为这里不但有银行、超市、医院和邮局，而且还有公园、餐馆和电影院。要是(yàoshi/if)有朋友(péngyou/friend)来，他们不但有吃饭的地方，还有玩儿的地方。这里离波士顿(Bōshìdùn/Boston)很近，去看球赛，去中国城，都很容易。我喜欢住在这里，因为这里不但方便，而且安静。

1) "我"住在哪儿？
   Ⓐ 美国西北部　　　　　　　Ⓑ 中国东北部
   Ⓒ 美国东北部　　　　　　　Ⓓ 中国东南部　　　（　　）

LESSON 5 DISCOVERING THE COMMUNITY

2) "我"住的社区里<u>没有</u>什么?
   Ⓐ 邮局　　　　　　　　　　Ⓑ 超市
   Ⓒ 餐馆　　　　　　　　　　Ⓓ 警察局　　　　　　(　　)

3) 你和朋友在社区里可以(kěyǐ/can)做什么?
   Ⓐ 游泳　　　　　　　　　　Ⓑ 看电影
   Ⓒ 看医生　　　　　　　　　Ⓓ 买书　　　　　　　(　　)

4) "我"为什么喜欢住在这里?
   Ⓐ 因为这里不但安静,而且方便。
   Ⓑ 因为这里不但离纽约很近,而且很安静。
   Ⓒ 因为这里不但可以吃饭,而且可以去看球赛。
   Ⓓ 因为这里不但可以去波士顿的中国城,而且可以看电影。　　　　(　　)

Writing

1. Practice writing the following characters in the correct stroke order.

不 不 不 不
但 但 但 但 但 但 但

不但

而 而 而 而 而 而
且 且 且 且 且

而且

社 社 社 社 社 社
区 区 区 区

社区

局 局局局局局局局
店 店店店店店店店店
馆 馆馆馆馆馆馆馆馆馆馆馆

2. What facilities does your community have? What facilities does your community not have? Answer in full sentences using 不但…而且…. Write at least six sentences.

___
___
___
___
___
___

3. Study the map of the community below. Describe it to a friend by writing an email talking about its facilities and their locations. You may start by saying whether this community is a convenient place to live in.

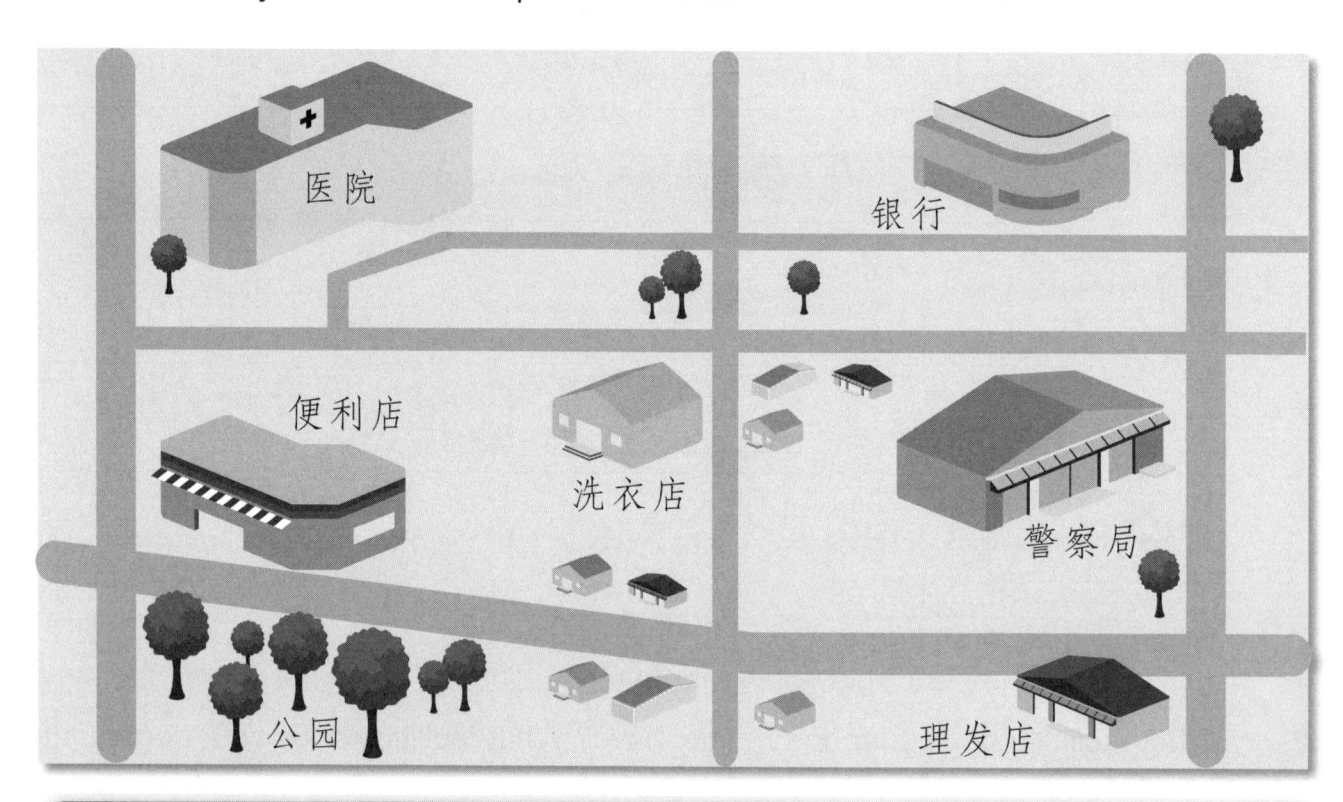

医院　银行
便利店　洗衣店　警察局
公园　理发店

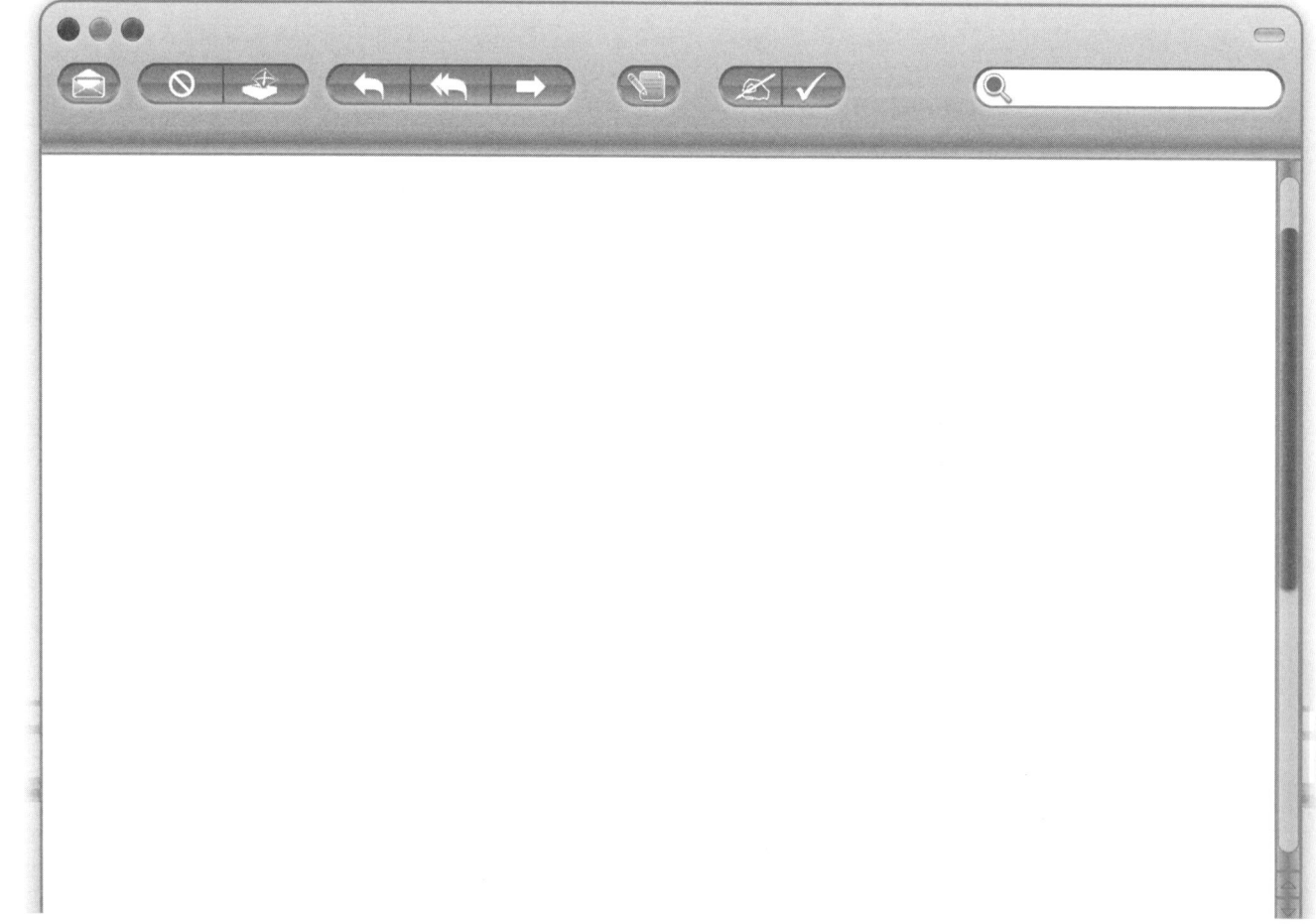

STEP 2 GETTING AROUND THE COMMUNITY

Listening

1. Listen to the dialog and answer the question.

   QUESTION: Which letter on the map represents the bank? (You are located at the star facing east.)

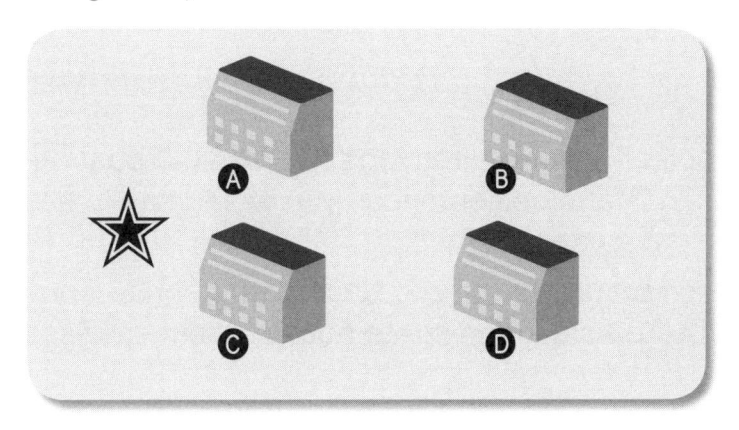

   (   )

2. You are in the street right outside the hairdresser's salon. Listen to and follow the instructions, and see what place you reach.

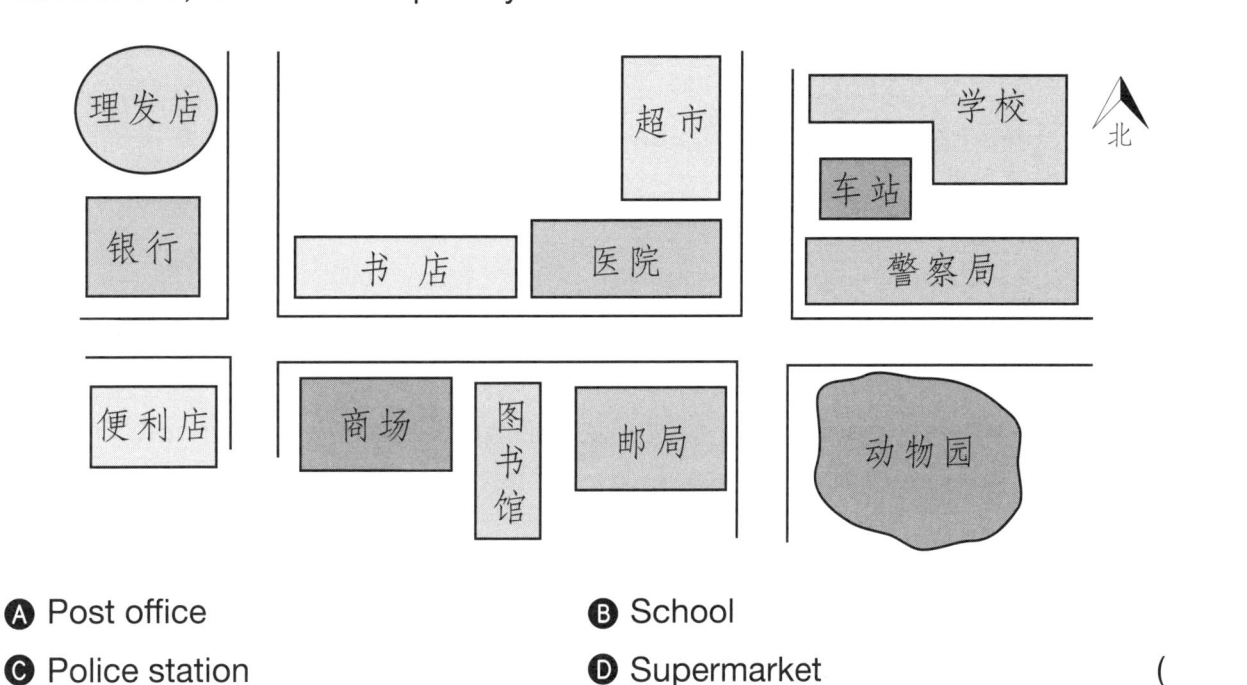

   Ⓐ Post office   **Ⓑ** School
   Ⓒ Police station   **Ⓓ** Supermarket   (   )

3. Listen to the dialog and determine whether the following statements are true (T) or false (F).

   Ⓐ The woman wants to know how to go to the post office.   (   )
   Ⓑ The woman must turn right at the first traffic light.   (   )
   Ⓒ The woman will pass two traffic lights before reaching the
   destination.   (   )

LESSON 5 DISCOVERING THE COMMUNITY

4. Listening rejoinder. Listen to the question and choose the most appropriate response.

   Ⓐ 我家离学校不远。

   Ⓑ 银行离书店有200码。

   Ⓒ 银行离邮局有100码。

   Ⓓ 银行离警察局有一英里。   (   )

Speaking

1. How would you politely ask for directions to a bank, a post office, and a convenience store? State the sentences you would say to ask someone.

2. How do you give directions to the zoo based on the map from Question 2 in the Listening Section? (You are in the street outside the hairdresser's salon.)

3. Research online to find out the distance from your home to (1) your school, (2) the nearest supermarket, (3) the nearest restaurant, and (4) the nearest movie theater. Prepare a 1-minute talk on whether or not it is convenient to live in your community.

4. Work with a classmate to create a short dialog on asking and giving directions using a map of your neighborhood. Present the dialog to the class.

Reading

1. Read the road sign, and write a sentence telling the distance from here (imagine you are located just under the sign) to 甘霖.

嵊州 SHENGZHOU 5km
甘霖 Ganlin 2km

2. Read the road signs from China and match each of them with the right meaning.

1) 2) 3) 4) 5) 6)

A) 直行和右转 C) 直行和左转 E) 右转
B) 左转 D) 向左和右转 F) 直行

3. Read the instructions and track the route on the grid area below. Start at point A in the grid. One square represents one mile. What shape do you get?

向东一直走，三英里以后，向南走，六英里以后向右拐，六英里以后向北走，三英里以后，向右拐，三英里以后向左拐，往前一直走三英里。

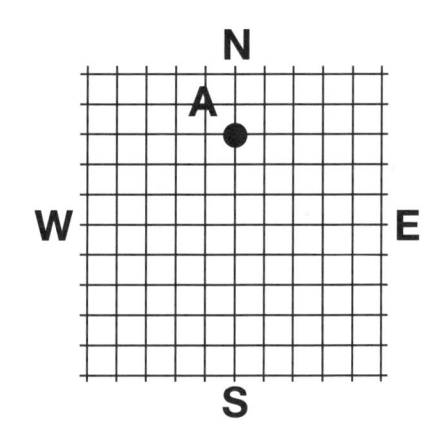

4. Read the email and answer the questions.

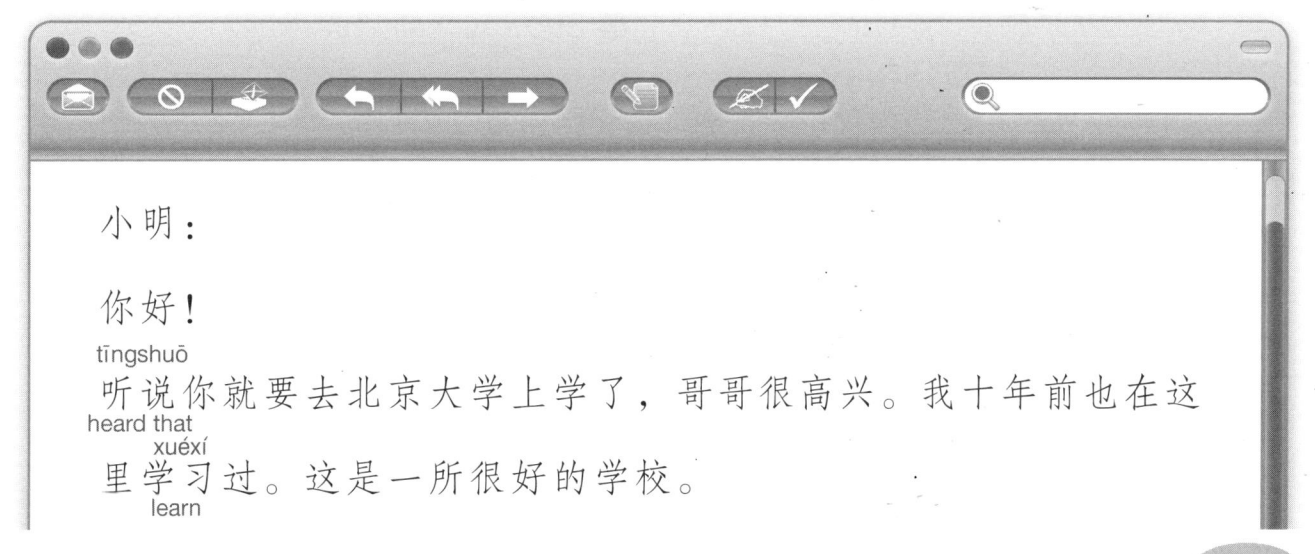

小明：

你好！

tīngshuō
听说你就要去北京大学上学了，哥哥很高兴。我十年前也在这
heard that
       xuéxí
里学习过。这是一所很好的学校。
    learn

LESSON 5 DISCOVERING THE COMMUNITY

你到北京以后，在北京火车站先坐地铁二号线，在西直门下车，
然后换地铁13号线，在五道口下车，出地铁，再坐公交车307
路，到中关园下车。下车以后，一直往前走，走200米后往右
拐，北大的大门就在你的前边。你会看到很多学生和一个
美丽的校园！

祝你一路顺风！

大伟

1. What school did Dawei go to ten years ago?
   A Beijing University   **B** Qinghai University
   C Jiaotong University   **D** New York University   (   )

2. How will Xiaoming travel to Beijing?
   A Plane   **B** Train
   C Subway   **D** Bus   (   )

3. What are the modes of transportation Xiaoming needs to take after arriving in Beijing?
   A Subway-bus-bike-walk   **B** Subway-subway-bus-walk
   C Subway-bus-taxi-walk   **D** Subway-walk-bus-walk   (   )

4. After he gets off the bus, how does he get to his school?
   A Walks straight ahead and turns left, the school is on his left.
   B Walks straight ahead and turns right, the school is on his right.
   C Walks straight ahead and turns right, the school is in front of him.
   D Walks straight ahead and the school is right in front of him.   (   )

Writing

1. Practice writing the following characters in the correct stroke order.

请 请 请 请 请 请 请 请 请
问 问 问 问 问 问

请问

往 往 往 往 往 往 往 往

往

向 向 向 向 向 向

向

拐 拐 拐 拐 拐 拐 拐 拐

拐

再 再 再 再 再 再

再

然 然 然 然 然 然 然 然 然 然 然 然
后 后 后 后 后 后

然后

LESSON 5 DISCOVERING THE COMMUNITY

就

一直

2. Fill in the blanks with the adverbs 先, 再, 然后 or 最后.

从这里到图书馆不远，你（　　　　）往北走，在第二个红绿灯向左拐，（　　　　）往西走二十米，（　　　　）往右拐，（　　　　）往前走50米就到图书馆了。

3. Your friend is going to travel to Beijing. However, he doesn't speak Chinese. Help him prepare a few sentences on asking for directions to the following places:

1) The Forbidden City (故宫)
_____

2) The Great Wall (长城)
_____

3) The Temple of Heaven (天坛)
_____

4) The Summer Palace (颐和园)
_____

STEP UP WITH CHINESE 2

5) The Silk Market (秀水街)

_____

4. Find out the distances between the following places. Write down the distances according to the unit of length indicated below.

   1) Beijing to Shanghai (kilometers):
   _____

   2) New York to San Francisco (miles):
   _____

   3) Paris to London (miles):
   _____

   4) Your classroom to the washroom (yards):
   _____

   5) Your desk to the board (meters):
   _____

5. Write instructions on how to get to the nearest Chinese restaurant from your school or to your favorite park from your home. (You may want to research online first before you start writing.)

   _____

   _____

   _____

   _____

LESSON 5 DISCOVERING THE COMMUNITY

STEP 3 LIVING IN THE COMMUNITY

Listening

1. Lily has a telephone message. Listen and answer the question.
   QUESTION: What will Fangfang's mom do in the afternoon?
   - **Ⓐ** Withdraw some money from the bank and go to the supermarket to buy groceries.
   - **Ⓑ** Deposit some money in the bank and go to the convenience store to buy groceries.
   - **Ⓒ** Deposit some money in the bank and go to the supermarket to buy groceries.
   - **Ⓓ** None of the above.   (   )

2. Listen to the dialog and answer the question.
   QUESTION: What is the activity that the lady <u>will not</u> do this morning?
   - **Ⓐ** Fill up the car with gas
   - **Ⓑ** Shop for clothes
   - **Ⓒ** Get her hair cut
   - **Ⓓ** See the doctor   (   )

3. Listen and choose the place where this dialog occurs.
   - **Ⓐ** Bank
   - **Ⓑ** Drug store
   - **Ⓒ** Post office
   - **Ⓓ** Gas station   (   )

4. Listen to Mark's description of his community, and determine whether the following statements are true (T) or false (F).
   - **Ⓐ** There is no post office in Mark's community.   (   )
   - **Ⓑ** There are many restaurants in Mark's community.   (   )
   - **Ⓒ** There is a pharmacy near Mark's home.   (   )
   - **Ⓓ** The gas station is not far away from Mark's home.   (   )
   - **Ⓔ** The movie theater is far from Mark's home.   (   )

Speaking

1. Imagine you are new in town.
   - You want to mail a letter. How do you ask for directions to the nearest post office?
   - You plan to go to the movies. How do you ask for the location of the movie theater and the distance from your place to the theater?

2. Imagine you are traveling to these countries: Canada, U.K., and France. Which country would you go to first, which would you visit second, and which last? Give a short speech describing your travels.

3. Tell a classmate the things you did last Saturday. Include at least three places you went to in the community, and the things you did there.

Reading

1. Correct the following sentences with the phrases given below.

   1) 爸爸每个星期六去加油站买药。( )

   2) 妈妈每个星期天下午去菜市场洗衣服。( )

   3) 我每个星期三下午没有课，所以我就去洗衣店看医生。( )

   4) 妈妈今天带弟弟去诊所买菜，然后去药店取钱。( )

   5) 爷爷喜欢运动，每天吃过晚饭都要到公园寄信。( )

   Ⓐ 看医生　　Ⓑ 买菜　　Ⓒ 加油
   Ⓓ 洗衣服　　Ⓔ 散步　　Ⓕ 买药

2. Mary has a busy schedule on Friday afternoon. It is already 2:30 and her car is very, very low on gas. She probably has enough gas to drive about three miles. She must do all of the tasks below this afternoon. Use the information in the table to help her determine the order of her tasks. Number the tasks to indicate the order.

	加油站	药房	邮局	洗衣店	银行
Closing time	24小时 (xiǎoshí / hour)	7:00pm	3:00pm	24小时	3:30pm
Location	西边	北边	东边	南边	西边
Distance (from home)	1英里	4英里	0.5英里	0.5英里	3英里

( ) 买药

( ) 开户

( ) 洗衣服

( ) 加油

( ) 寄信

3. Study the map below and determine whether the statements are true (T) or false (F).

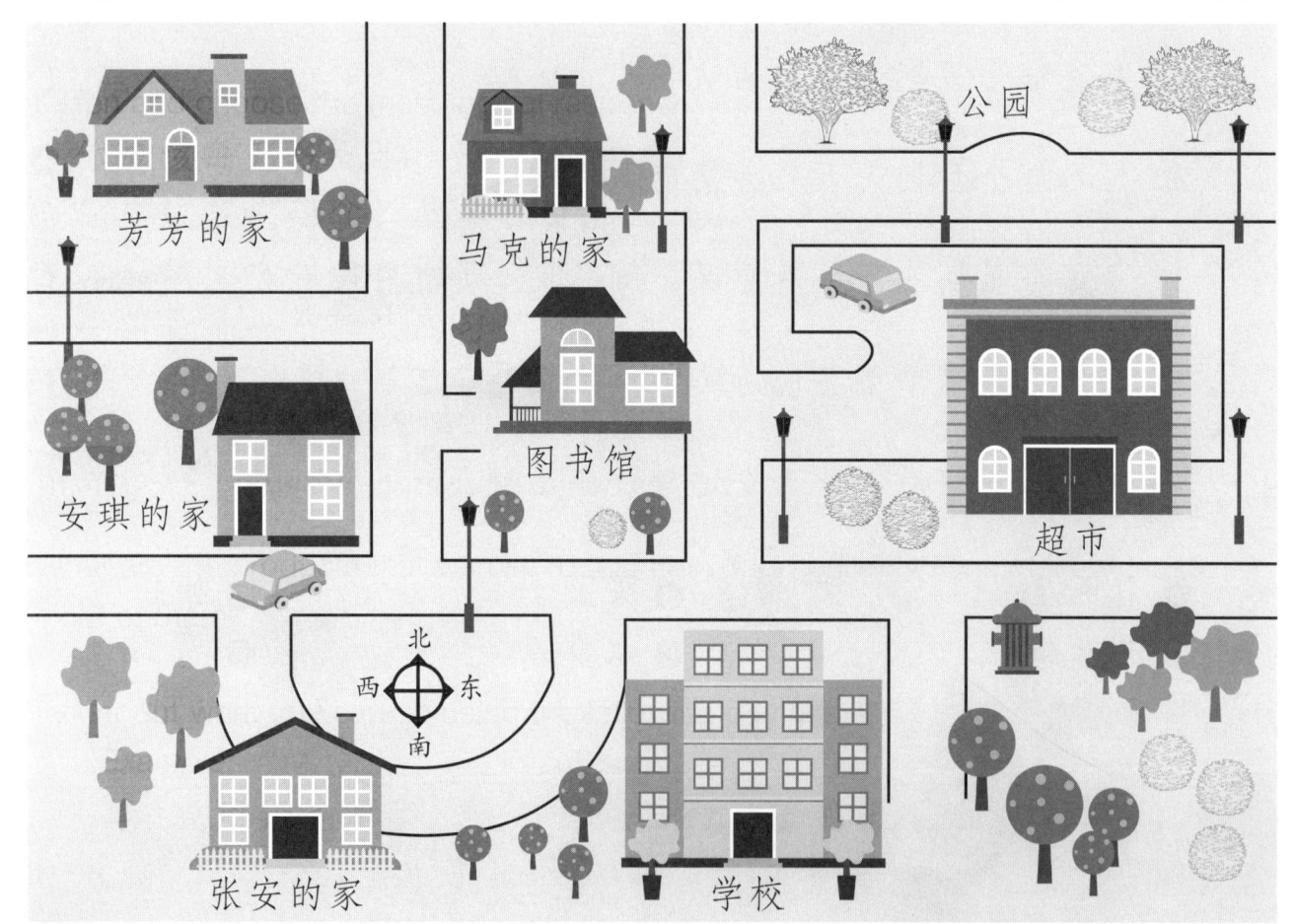

1) 公园在社区的西北边。　　　　　　　　　　　　　（　　）

2) 超市离学校不远。　　　　　　　　　　　　　　　（　　）

3) 超市外边有一个商场。　　　　　　　　　　　　　（　　）

4) 张安的家离学校最近。　　　　　　　　　　　　　（　　）

5) 安琪的家离学校最远。　　　　　　　　　　　　　（　　）

6) 从安琪家到图书馆，很方便。　　　　　　　　　　（　　）

7) 从马克的家去其他三个同学的家，你得先到芳芳的家，
   再到张安的家，然后到安琪的家。　　　　　　　　（　　）

4. Read Anqi's blog and number the tasks in the correct order.

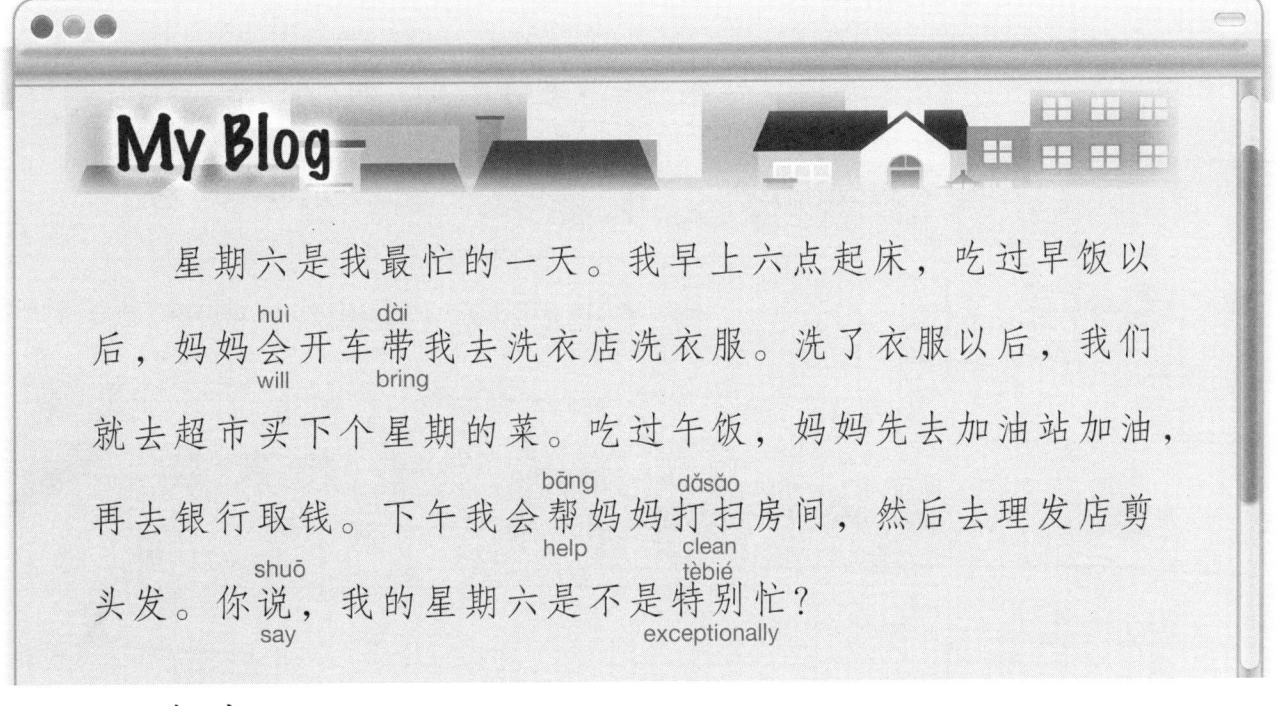

My Blog

星期六是我最忙的一天。我早上六点起床，吃过早饭以后，妈妈会开车带我去洗衣店洗衣服。洗了衣服以后，我们就去超市买下个星期的菜。吃过午饭，妈妈先去加油站加油，再去银行取钱。下午我会帮妈妈打扫房间，然后去理发店剪头发。你说，我的星期六是不是特别忙？

(　　) 加油
(　　) 剪头发
(　　) 洗衣服
(　　) 取钱
(　　) 买菜
(　　) 打扫房间

Writing

1. Practice writing the following characters in the correct stroke order.

购购购购购购购购
物物物物物物物物

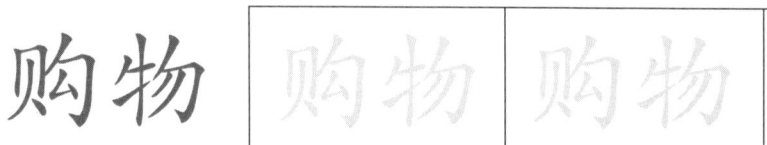

购物 | 购物 | 购物 | | |

寄寄寄寄寄寄寄寄寄寄寄
信信信信信信信信

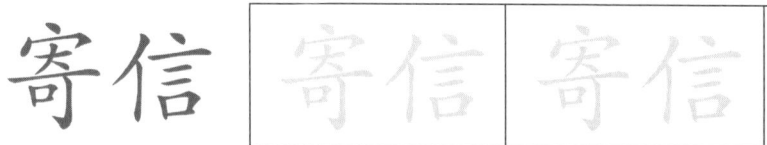

寄信 | 寄信 | 寄信 | | |

看看看看看看看看看
医医医医医医医
生生生生生

看医生 | 看医生 | | |

散散散散散散散散散散散散
步步步步步步步

散步 | 散步 | 散步 | | |

先先先先先先
先 | 先 | 先 | 先 | | | | |

2. List 8-10 activities you can do in your community.
   Example: 去菜场买菜，去餐馆吃饭

   _____
   _____
   _____
   _____
   _____

3. Give directions on how to get to the library from Zhang An's house.

   _____
   _____

LESSON 5 DISCOVERING THE COMMUNITY

4. Read Ding Qiang's daily routine in the morning. Using this as a guide, write what you often do in the evening between dinner and bedtime.

> 从星期一到星期五我每天早上6点起床。起床以后我先刷牙，再洗脸，然后穿衣服，最后吃早饭。吃过早饭以后，差不多(chàbuduō / about)7点，爸爸开车送我去上学。

5. Write an email to your e-pal describing your community. How do you like your community? What do you often do over the weekend in your community? What facilities do you have and what facilities are lacking in the community? Write at least 200 characters.

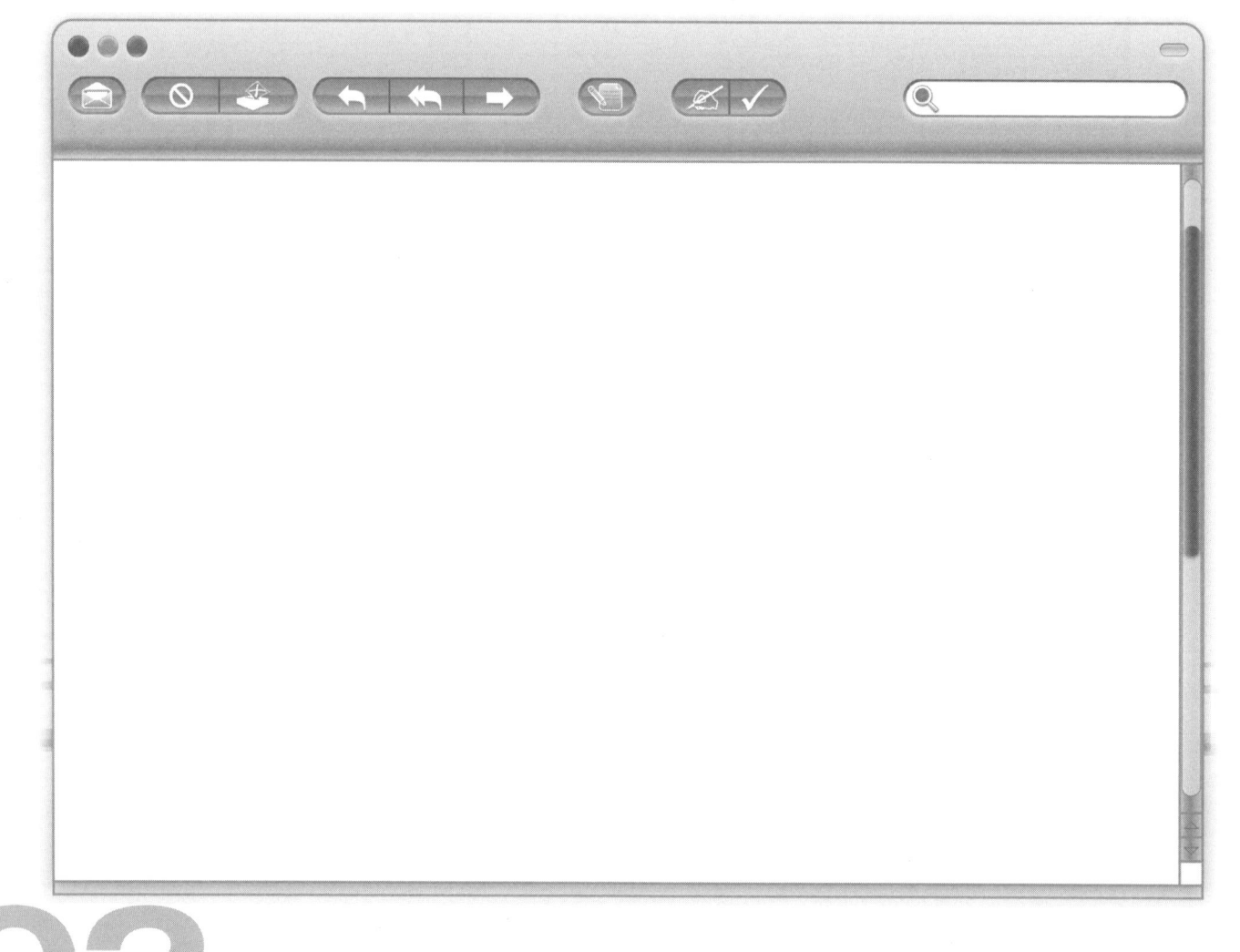

REVIEW 1 (Lessons 1 – 5)

Listening

1. Listen to the short dialog and answer the question.
   QUESTION: What do they need to wear tomorrow if they go outside?
   - Ⓐ 雨衣、雨伞
   - Ⓑ 羽绒服、手套
   - Ⓒ 衬衫、长裤
   - Ⓓ T恤、短裤   (   )

2. Listen to the short dialog and answer the question.
   QUESTION: What was not included in the Fangfang's job list yesterday afternoon?
   - Ⓐ 去银行
   - Ⓑ 去邮局
   - Ⓒ 洗衣服
   - Ⓓ 剪头发   (   )

3. Mark's mother is out running some errands. She leaves instructions for Mark to arrange some items in their new home. Listen and answer the question.
   QUESTION: Which one of the following statements is false?
   - Ⓐ 把画挂在墙上。
   - Ⓑ 把水果放在餐桌上。
   - Ⓒ 把书放在书架上。
   - Ⓓ 把花插在花瓶里。   (   )

4. Listen to a conversation and answer the three questions that follow.
   1) Where did Anqi go for summer?
      - Ⓐ 北京
      - Ⓑ 上海
      - Ⓒ 香港
      - Ⓓ 巴黎   (   )

   2) Which activity was not mentioned by Anqi in her summer camp?
      - Ⓐ 学中文
      - Ⓑ 学书法
      - Ⓒ 上补习班
      - Ⓓ 旅游   (   )

   3) On what date does this conversation probably take place?
      - Ⓐ 六月一号
      - Ⓑ 七月十五号
      - Ⓒ 八月十五号
      - Ⓓ 八月一号   (   )

5. Listen to a conversation and answer the three questions that follow.
   1) What modes of transportation does Mary take to go to her new school?
      Ⓐ 自行车和地铁　　　　Ⓑ 地铁和走路
      Ⓒ 地铁和公交车　　　　Ⓓ 公交车和走路　　　　　　　(　　)

   2) Why does Mary change her school?
      Ⓐ 她不喜欢她以前的学校。
      Ⓑ 她喜欢去东边的学校。
      Ⓒ 她的家搬到了北京的东边。
      Ⓓ 她的家搬到了北京的西边。　　　　　　　　　　　　(　　)

   3) How is Mary's new school like?
      Ⓐ 很大，也很新　　　　Ⓑ 很小，离她家很远
      Ⓒ 很不方便，人也很多　Ⓓ 很大，离她家很近　　　　　(　　)

Speaking

1. Talk about one of your favorite souvenirs, including where you got it, when you got it, how you got it, etc., using the 是…的 structure.

2. What is your favorite place in the world? Report today's weather in your current place and the weather in your favorite place, as well as what people wear in the current season in these two places.

3. What are the things you plan to do on Saturday morning? In what order do you plan to do those things? Use 先, 再, and 然后.

4. Compare the neighborhood around your school with the one around your home. Talk about the facilities in both areas and the advantages and disadvantages of living in the two neighborhoods using 不但…而且… and 因为…所以….

5. Imagine that you need to rearrange your room. How would you want to change it? Talk about five things you would want to do, using the 把 structure.

Reading

1. Read the paragraph and determine whether the following statements are true (T) or false (T).

新学年又要开始了！今年对马克来说是全新的一年。因为马克的爸爸要在中国工作，所以他会在中国北京的国际学校上高中十年级。马克的爸爸是五月到北京的，然后买了新房子，七月时把家搬到了北京。马克和妈妈、妹妹是七月二十号来北京的，还带来了他们的宠物狗。马克很喜欢他们的新房子。他们的新家在北京的东北部，离市中心不太远，很方便。社区很安静，也很漂亮。但是马克不太开心，因为他没有朋友，他很想念美国的同学。虽然他学过两年中文，会说一些中文，但是他还是觉得和北京人聊天很难。他们说的话和他学的中文不一样！后来，马克参加了一个中文夏令营，中文进步了很多，而且认识了好几个新朋友！快要开学了，马克很兴奋。

1) 今年马克会在北京上学。 (　　)
2) 因为马克的爸爸要在中国工作，所以他一家人都搬到了中国。 (　　)
3) 马克不喜欢北京，因为他不喜欢他的新家。 (　　)
4) 马克学过中文。 (　　)
5) 马克觉得和北京人聊天很容易。 (　　)

2. Read the email and answer the questions.

小明：

你好！

我已经在美国的新学校上学了。因为开学太忙了，所以没时间写信给你。我的学校在美国东北的一个小镇。这里离纽约只有二十英里。镇里有火车，去纽约和波士顿都很方便。这个学校很大，也很漂亮。教学楼都是红色的砖房，白色的窗户。楼外种着大片的绿草地和美丽的鲜花。我的宿舍在二楼，不大，但是放一张床、一张桌子和一个衣柜是没问题的。我把以前的照片贴在了墙上。这样我就可以常常看见我的老朋友了。

这里的同学和老师都很友好。学校餐厅的美国菜也不错。

你的新学期也很忙吧？上海还很热吗？要过中秋节了吧？有时间给我写信！

祝好！

李春雨
二零一三年九月二十五日

1) 李春雨现在在哪里上学？

___

2) 从李春雨的新学校去附近的大城市方便吗？怎么去？
   (fùjìn - nearby)

___

3) 李春雨的学校里有什么？

___

4) 李春雨的宿舍里有什么家具？

___

5) 在中国，九月底、十月初常常要过哪个节日？
   (dǐ - end, chū - beginning, festival)

___

3. Read the text exchanges and answer the questions.

> 丁强：你在上海还好吗？

> 玛丽：还不错，上海很美，但是我不太喜欢这里的天气，常常下雨，有点儿冷。

> 丁强：是吗？北京今天是二十八度，特别热。
> (tèbié - exceptionally)

> 玛丽：上海只有二十度，还下着小雨，比北京冷多了！

> 丁强：那你得多穿点儿衣服！把毛衣穿上吧。

玛丽：我穿着毛衣呢，还穿了一件风衣。
ne
windbreaker

丁强：我今天只穿了一条长裤和一件衬衫，出去还得戴太阳镜，外面热极了！
zhǐ
just

玛丽：才五月就这么热了，像是夏天了。
cái only
xiàng just like

丁强：对，我不太喜欢北京的夏天，北京的秋天最好！

玛丽：是啊，今年秋天我要回北京工作了。

丁强：太好了，你回来以后，我们一起去爬山！
yìqǐ
together

1) What aspect of Shanghai did Mary dislike?
   A 上海人　　　　　　　　　**B** 上海的房子
   C 上海的天气　　　　　　　**D** 上海的夏天　　　　　　（　）

2) How was Shanghai's weather at the time of their chat?
   A 晴，热　　　　　　　　　**B** 下雨，热
   C 下雨，冷　　　　　　　　**D** 晴，冷　　　　　　　　（　）

3) How was Beijing's weather at the time of their chat?
   A 晴，热　　　　　　　　　**B** 下雨，热
   C 下雨，冷　　　　　　　　**D** 晴，冷　　　　　　　　（　）

4) What did Mary wear today?
   A 短裙　　　　　　　　　　**B** 长衣、长裤
   C 毛衣、风衣　　　　　　　**D** 衬衫、西裤　　　　　　（　）

5) What did Ding Qiang wear today?
   - Ⓐ 短裤、T恤
   - Ⓑ 衬衫、长裤
   - Ⓒ 毛衣、风衣
   - Ⓓ 衬衫、牛仔裤   (   )

6) What is the best season in Beijing according to Ding Qiang?
   - Ⓐ 春天
   - Ⓑ 夏天
   - Ⓒ 秋天
   - Ⓓ 冬天   (   )

4. Read the map and match the questions with the directions.

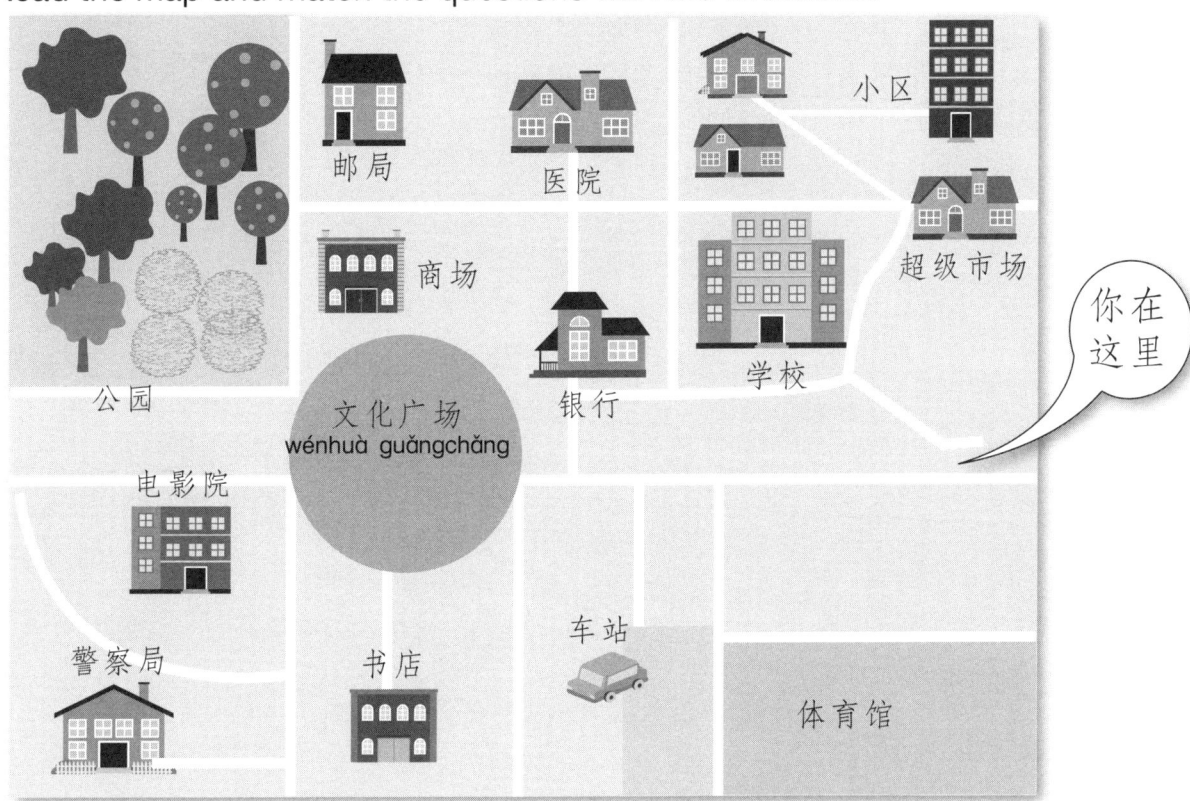

（Map: 公园、邮局、医院、小区、商场、超级市场、学校、文化广场 wénhuà guǎngchǎng、电影院、银行、你在这里、警察局、书店、车站、体育馆）

1) 请问，去车站怎么走？
2) 请问，这里离邮局有多远？
3) 请问，这个社区有银行吗？
4) 请问，电影院在哪儿？
5) 请问，这条街(jiē, street)上有没有图书馆？

Ⓐ 一直往前走，过了文化广场，你就看到了。
Ⓑ 往前走，在第二个路口往左拐。
Ⓒ 没有，但是这里有一个书店，你往前走，在文化广场往左拐就到了。
Ⓓ 很远，你要往前走，在第三个路口往右拐，过了银行以后，在医院的路口往左拐。
Ⓔ 有，往前走，在第三个路口往右拐。

REVIEW 1 (LESSONS 1–5)

Writing

1. Design a school and town campus with a high school where 500 students live on campus. Draw a map with at least eight different facilities and mark their names in Chinese.

2. Find out the weather for the next five days and complete the table below. An example has been done for you.

日期	五月二十日，星期一					
天气	晴					
气温	摄氏28–30度					
衣服	短衣短裤					

3. Complete the following sentences.

   1) 因为我家离学校很近，_____。

   2) 餐桌上放着一些水果，_____。

   3) 我的社区里不但有便利店，_____。

   4) 我先去银行存款，_____。

   5) _____，所以我没做作业。

4. Based on the following summer report chart, write an email to your friend 文中 in China telling him about your summer. (Write at least 250 characters.)

日期	六月一号到十五号	七月一号到三十号	八月一号到十五号
Location	美国加州 (Jiāzhōu California) 到纽约	中国北京大学	美国纽约中国城
Activity	搬家、打扫 (dǎsǎo clean) 房子	中文夏令营	中国文化博物馆 (wénhuà bówùguǎn Cultural Museum) 做义工
How I feel	累、忙、有意思	兴奋、开心	喜欢、高兴

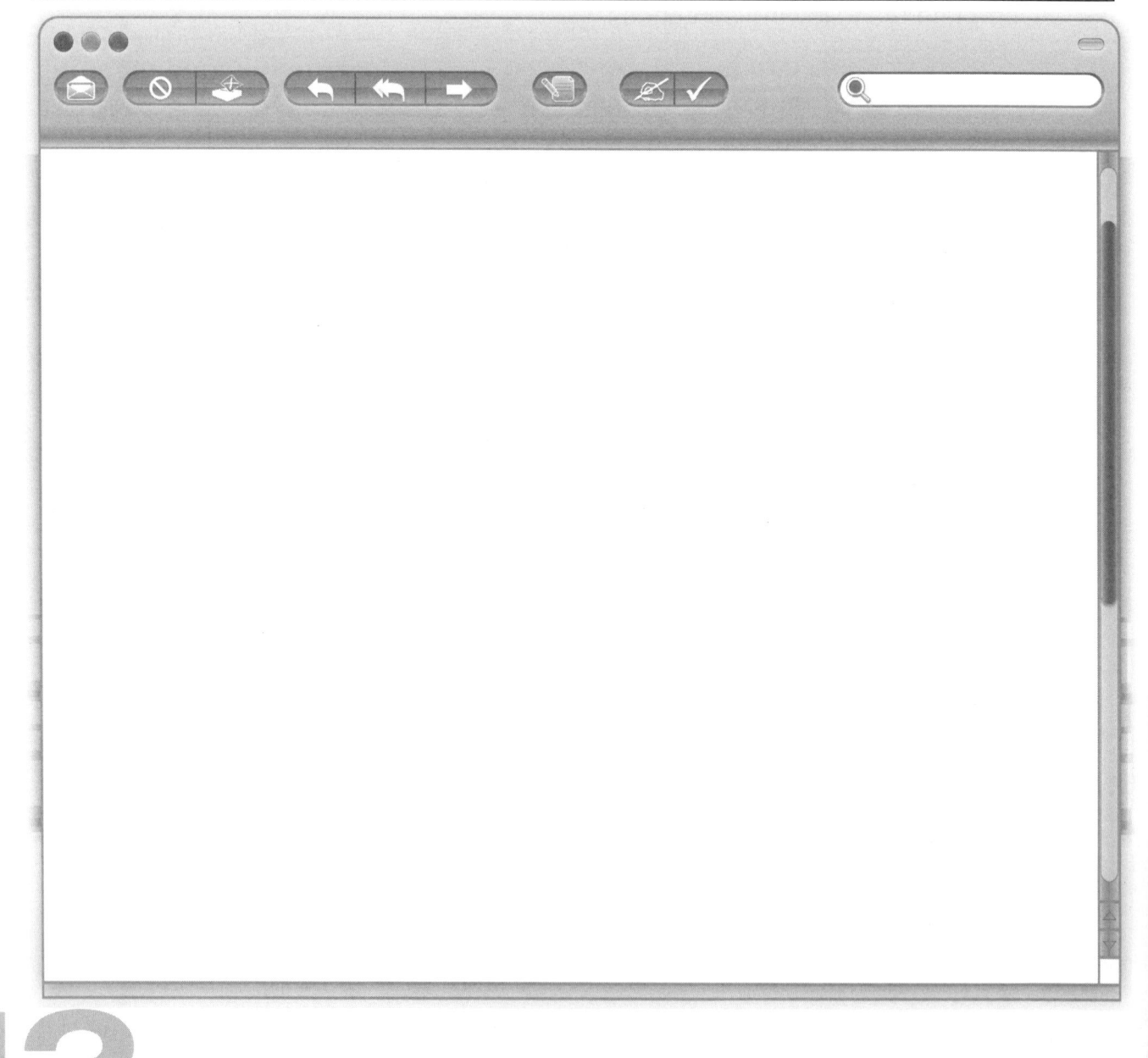

LESSON 6 MEETING NEW PEOPLE

STEP 1 EXPLORING PROFESSIONS

Listening

1. Listen to the question and choose the most appropriate response.
   - Ⓐ 我爸爸五十岁。
   - Ⓑ 我妈妈也是老师。
   - Ⓒ 我爸爸喜欢唱歌。
   - Ⓓ 我爸爸是工程师。   （   ）

2. Listen to the questions and choose the response that answers both questions.
   - Ⓐ 我和哥哥都是中国人。我们住在北京。
   - Ⓑ 我哥哥是医生，在医院工作。
   - Ⓒ 我哥哥在书店工作，离我们的家很远。
   - Ⓓ 哥哥是一个发型师，他很喜欢他的工作。   （   ）

3. Listen to the description and answer the question.
   QUESTION: 他是做什么工作的？
   - Ⓐ 医生
   - Ⓑ 厨师
   - Ⓒ 发型师
   - Ⓓ 售货员   （   ）

4. Listen to the dialog and answer the question.
   QUESTION: Where did this conversation take place?
   - Ⓐ 银行
   - Ⓑ 商场
   - Ⓒ 饭店
   - Ⓓ 理发店   （   ）

Speaking

1. Introduce your family members and their professions.

2. Ask a classmate what his or her family members' professions are and where they work. Fill in the information in the table below. If you or your classmate do not have some of these people in your family, imagine you do and give them a profession.

家人	爸爸	妈妈	哥哥	姐姐		
工作						
工作地点 location						

3. Imagine that you know the people in the pictures personally. Give them a name and talk about their profession and their place of work.

4. Answer the following questions in Chinese: What profession would you like to have in the future and why? Where would you like to work and why?

STEP UP WITH CHINESE 2

Reading

1. Match the celebrities with their professions. Search online if you do not know them.

   1) I. M. Pei
   2) Vera Wang
   3) Sam Walton
   4) Yo-yo Ma
   5) Ziyi Zhang
   6) Thomas Edison
   7) Liping Yang
   8) J.P. Morgan

   Ⓐ 银行家
   Ⓑ 舞蹈家
   Ⓒ 建筑师
   Ⓓ 音乐家
   Ⓔ 服装设计师
   Ⓕ 演员
   Ⓖ 科学家
   Ⓗ 商人

2. Match the following items and make sentences in the spaces provided.

   1) 厨师
   2) 记者
   3) 运动员
   4) 农民
   5) 音乐家

   A) 在舞台 (stage) 上
   B) 在体育馆里
   C) 在农田里
   D) 在报社里
   E) 在餐馆里

   i) 做饭
   ii) 种玉米
   iii) 表演
   iv) 比赛
   v) 写稿件 (gǎojiàn, articles)

   Sentence 1: _____

   Sentence 2: _____

   Sentence 3: _____

   Sentence 4: _____

   Sentence 5: _____

3. Number the following sentences in the correct order to form a coherent paragraph.

(　) 我家人的爱好都不一样。
(　) 我将来想当一个电脑工程师。
(　) 她喜欢听音乐。
(　) 他常常在他的画室里工作。
(　) 我妈妈是会计师。
(　) 我最喜欢数学和电脑。
(　) 他常常在操场踢球。
(　) 我爸爸喜欢画画，是一个画家。
(　) 我哥哥喜欢运动。
(　) 他是足球运动员。
(　) 她最爱的音乐家是贝多芬(Bèiduōfēn/Beethoven)，最喜欢的歌手是后街男孩(Hòujiē Nánhái/Backstreet Boys)。
(　) 我是一个高中生。

Writing

1. Practice writing the following characters in the correct stroke order.

工 工 工
作 作 作 作 作 作 作

工作

商 商 商 商 商 商 商 商 商 商
店 店 店 店 店 店 店 店

商店

餐餐餐餐餐餐餐餐餐餐餐餐餐餐餐
馆馆馆馆馆馆馆馆馆馆馆

餐馆 | 餐馆 | 餐馆 | | |

发发发发发
廊廊廊廊廊廊廊廊廊廊

发廊 | 发廊 | 发廊 | | |

2. Fill in the blanks with the appropriate characters to form the words for different professions.

1) _____ 师   4) _____ 师   7) _____ 师   10) _____ 师

2) _____ 员   5) _____ 员   8) _____ 员   11) _____ 员

3) _____ 家   6) _____ 家   9) _____ 家   12) _____ 家

3. Write a sentence for each of the pictures below.

1)  *Example:* 教师在学校里工作。

2) _____

3) _____

LESSON 6 MEETING NEW PEOPLE

4) _____ 5) _____ 6) _____

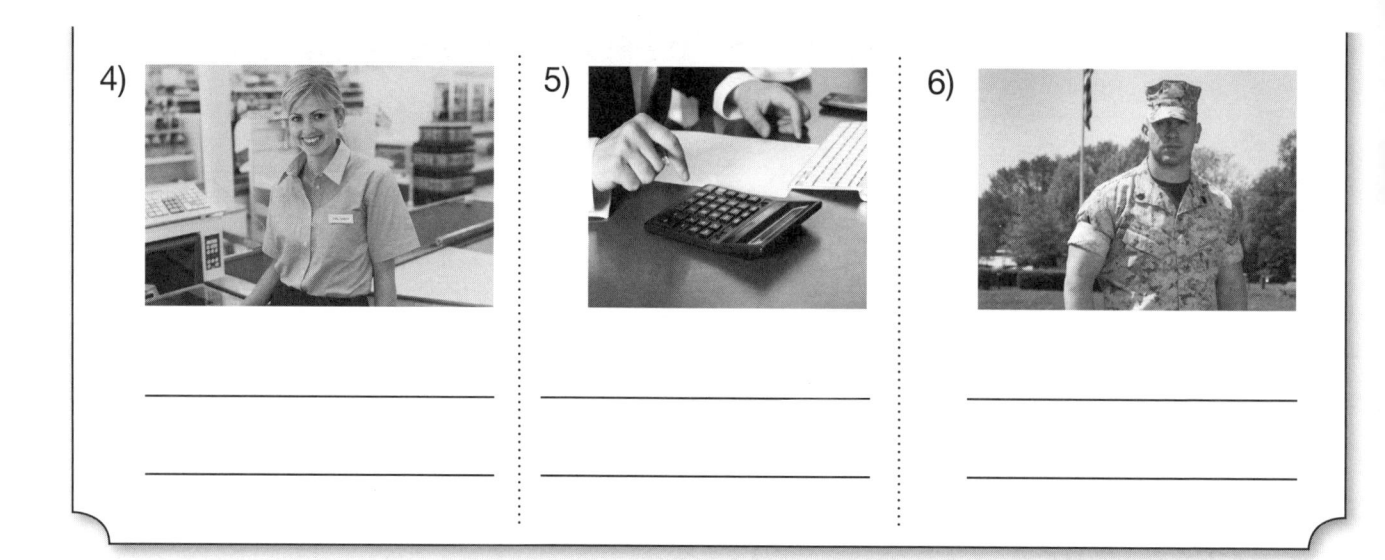

4. Use the following information from 安琪's English résumé and write a paragraph about her in Chinese, using 从…到…, 当, 在, and 做.

1993-1997	Beijing No. 10 School	high school student
1997-2001	Medical School of Beijing University	college student
2001-2008	Beijing No.1 People's Hospital	doctor
2008-present	New York University	professor

STEP 2 FINDING ONE'S ASPIRATIONS

Listening

1. Listen to the dialog and choose the most appropriate response.
   - Ⓐ 我妈妈要去超市买菜。
   - Ⓑ 我打算去电影院看电影。
   - Ⓒ 明天天气不好！
   - Ⓓ 我舅舅明天要来我的家。 (   )

2. Listen to the dialog and answer the question.
   QUESTION: 为什么张安将来不想当医生？
   - Ⓐ 因为他爸爸妈妈都当医生。
   - Ⓑ 因为当医生很舒服。
   - Ⓒ 因为当医生很累，也很忙。
   - Ⓓ 因为他喜欢当画家。 (   )

3. Listen to the dialog and answer the question.
   QUESTION: 丁强打算在什么行业工作？
   - Ⓐ 建筑业
   - Ⓑ 艺术界
   - Ⓒ 教育界
   - Ⓓ 旅游业 (   )

4. Listen and choose the most appropriate response.
   - Ⓐ 对，我写得好。
   - Ⓑ 我不喜欢写作。
   - Ⓒ 不，我想当记者。
   - Ⓓ 我哥哥打算当作家。 (   )

Speaking

1. Answer the following questions in Chinese:
   What field do you plan to go into in the future? Why?
   What job do you plan to have? Why?

2. Interview three of your classmates about their plans for future professions and the fields they want to go into. Then share your answers with others.

同学			
将来的工作			
将来的行业			

3. Pick three professions that you would like to do in the future and talk about what you would do in those professions. Use 如果…就….

4. Pick three famous people that you do not like and talk about what you would change if you were that person.

Reading

1. Match the companies with the correct industries.

   1) Google   Ⓐ 医药业
   2) Coca Cola   Ⓑ 金融业
   3) CNN   Ⓒ 信息业
   4) American Express Ⓓ 食品业
   5) Emirates   Ⓔ 新闻业
   6) Tylenol   Ⓕ 旅游业

2. Match the following interests with the related fields of work.

1) 画画
2) 写作
3) 跑步
4) 服装设计
5) 唱歌
6) 表演
7) 辩论 (biànlùn, debate)

Ⓐ 法律界
Ⓑ 音乐界
Ⓒ 娱乐界
Ⓓ 艺术界
Ⓔ 文学界
Ⓕ 体育界
Ⓖ 时尚界

3. Complete the dialog by choosing the correct option for each blank from the choices below.

马克： 芳芳，你的钢琴弹得真好！

芳芳： _____

马克： 谢谢，我将来打算当一个歌手。你想当钢琴家吗？

芳芳： _____

马克： 那，你打算在什么行业工作？

芳芳： _____

马克： 真的吗？我姐姐也是服装设计师！
       zhēnde
       really

芳芳： _____

马克： 好啊，欢迎你来我家！

Ⓐ 我会在时尚界工作，当一个服装设计师。

Ⓑ 太好了，我以后可以来你家和她聊天、学习吗？
   tài   kěyǐ   xuéxí
   too   can   learn

Ⓒ 不，我不想。

Ⓓ 谢谢！你的歌唱得也很好啊！

4. Read the paragraph and determine whether the following statements are true (T) or false (F).

> 我家有四口人，我们住在纽约。我爸爸是一个消防员，他的消防队(duì team)就在我们的社区里。我爸爸工作很努力，虽然(suīrán although)工作危险(wēixiǎn dangerous)，但是(dànshì but)，他很喜欢他的工作。我妈妈是一个医生，给(for)人们看牙，治牙病。她是一个很好的牙医，她觉得在医药业工作很好。我和哥哥都是学生。我喜欢看新闻，也喜欢写作。将来，我打算当一名记者，报道新闻。我哥哥喜欢画画和建筑，他将来可能会做一个建筑设计师。

1) 我家里有一个人在医药业工作。 ( )
2) 我哥哥是一名建筑设计师。 ( )
3) 我喜欢看新闻，也喜欢写作。 ( )
4) 我妈妈觉得她的行业很好。 ( )
5) 我爸爸不喜欢他的工作，因为太危险了。 ( )
6) 我哥哥的爱好是画画。 ( )

Writing

1. Practice writing the following characters in the correct stroke order.

打 打 打 打 打
算 算 算 算 算 算 算 算 算 算 算 算

打算 | 打算 | 打算 | | |

行行行行行行
业业业业业

行业 | 行业 | 行业 | | |

会会会会会会

会 | 会 | 会 | 会 | | | | | |

可可可可可
能能能能能能能能能能

可能 | 可能 | 可能 | | |

如如如如如如
果果果果果果果果

如果 | 如果 | 如果 | | |

2. Fill in the blanks with a description of what each profession does.

1) 医生的工作是 _____

2) 音乐家的工作是 _____

3) 消防员的工作是 _____

4) 记者的工作是 _____

5) 军人的工作是 _____

6) 建筑师的工作是 _____

3. Answer the questions based on your personal life.

1) 你将来打算在什么行业工作？
_____

2) 你将来打算做什么工作？
_____

3) 你最喜欢哪个行业？为什么？
_____

4) 你最喜欢什么工作？为什么？
_____

4. Complete the following sentences with logical information.

1) 如果我打球打得好，_____

2) 如果他有时间，_____

3) 如果爸爸会做很好吃的菜，_____

4) 如果明天天气好，_____

5) 如果中国离美国不远，_____

6) _____ ，我就会设计最漂亮的大楼。
   piàoliang / beautiful

7) _____ ，我就会努力医治病人。

8) _____ ，你的身体就会很健康。

5. Write an email to your e-pal in China on the topic of professions. Describe your family members' professions, as well as your interests, hobbies, and future aspirations. Use as many new vocabulary words as possible. Feel free to use an online dictionary for any new vocabulary you might need. Write at least 250 characters.

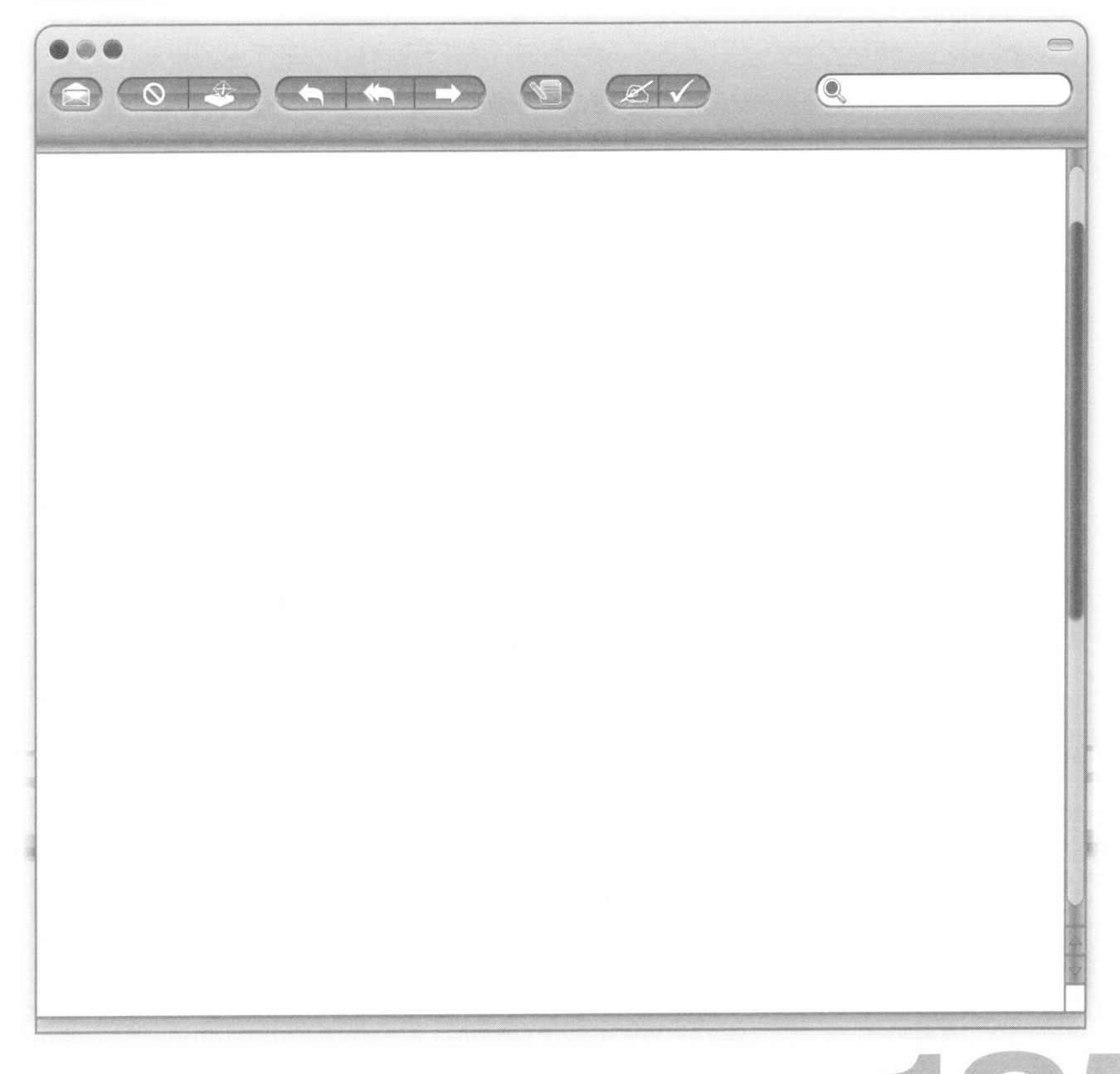

STEP 3 DISCOVERING FAMOUS PEOPLE

Listening

1. Listen to the introduction and answer the question.
   QUESTION: 李娜在什么行业工作？
   - Ⓐ 网球
   - Ⓑ 体育
   - Ⓒ 娱乐
   - Ⓓ 食品   (   )

2. Listen to the dialog and choose the most appropriate response.
   - Ⓐ 表演
   - Ⓑ 画画
   - Ⓒ 唱歌
   - Ⓓ 篮球   (   )

3. Listen to the dialog and choose the most appropriate response to answer the question.
   QUESTION: 安琪将来比较可能在哪个行业工作？
   - Ⓐ 数学
   - Ⓑ 科学
   - Ⓒ 艺术
   - Ⓓ 文学   (   )

4. Listen and answer the question.
   QUESTION: 这个人在哪些方面很有成就？
   (There is more than one correct answer.)
   - Ⓐ 科学
   - Ⓑ 音乐
   - Ⓒ 体育
   - Ⓓ 写作   (   )

5. Listen to the dialog and answer the question.
   QUESTION: What traits does Ms. Li possess?
   - Ⓐ 勇敢、友善、认真
   - Ⓑ 孝顺、有学问、认真
   - Ⓒ 有学问、友善、认真
   - Ⓓ 风趣、友善、伟大   (   )

Speaking

1. Talk about the areas you and your family members are talented in.

2. Search online for the following Chinese people and talk about their areas of achievement.

> Jay Chow; Li Na; Mo Yan; Ai Weiwei; Yang Liping

3. Who is the greatest president in your opinion? Comment briefly on that person, using 不仅…还….

4. Record a one-minute description of your favorite celebrity, including information such as gender, age, nationality, profession, field of work, achievements, personality traits, etc. Do not mention his or her name. Share it with your classmates and see if they can guess who it is.

Reading

1. Read the sentences below and select the right person that fits the description.

    1) 他不仅功夫(gōngfu/Kungfu)好，还很风趣。　　　　　　　　　　　　（　　）

    2) 她不仅勇敢，还很聪明。　　　　　　　　　　　　　　　　　　（　　）

    3) 他不仅在篮球方面很有成就，而且学习很努力。　　　　　　　　（　　）

    4) 她不仅滑冰滑得很好，而且在服装设计方面很有成就。　　　　　（　　）

    - **A** Vera Wang
    - **B** Jackie Chan
    - **C** Mulan
    - **D** Jeremy Lin

2. Choose the top five qualities that the following jobs require.

    > 正直，认真，负责，勤劳，风趣，友善，能干，勇敢，有创意，有恒心

    1) 建筑师：＿＿＿＿＿＿＿＿＿＿＿＿＿＿＿＿＿＿＿＿＿＿＿＿＿＿＿

    2) 律师：＿＿＿＿＿＿＿＿＿＿＿＿＿＿＿＿＿＿＿＿＿＿＿＿＿＿＿＿

3. Read the following paragraph and decide which job is more suitable for the person.

> 我的爱好很多，喜欢唱歌、画画、摄影(shèyǐng photography)、看电影。我最不喜欢的课是历史和英文。有空(yǒukòng free)的时候我喜欢在纽约的大街上骑自行车，看各种各样(gè zhǒng gè yàng all kinds of)的大楼、小街。有时候还会停(tíng stop)下来，画一画我喜欢的建筑。我觉得自己(zìjǐ oneself)不仅很有创意，做事情(shìqing thing, matter)也很认真、负责。我打算将来学习设计。我觉得将来在建筑设计方面会取得成就。

Ⓐ 新闻记者 Ⓑ 服装设计师
Ⓒ 建筑师 Ⓓ 会计   (　　)

4. Read the paragraph and answer the questions in Chinese.

> 贝聿铭(Bèi Yùmíng)是一位(wèi)很有成就的建筑设计大师。他出生在中国广州(Guǎngzhōu Guangzhou)，在香港和上海长大，十八岁到美国留学(liúxué study abroad)，学习建筑学。贝聿铭做事认真，有恒心，不怕困难(pà kùnnan afraid of difficulty)。贝聿铭在现代(xiàndài modern)建筑设计方面很有特长。他设计过很多有名的大楼，其中(qízhōng among them)香港中银大厦(Zhōngyín Dàshà Bank of China Tower)、北京香山饭店(Xiāngshān Fàndiàn Fragrant Hill Hotel)、法国罗浮宫金字塔(Luófúgóng Jīnzìtǎ Louvre Pyramid)，和美国肯尼迪总统图书馆(Kěnnídí Zǒngtǒng John F. Kennedy Presidential Library)都是伟大的建筑。人们觉得他设计的建筑不仅有创意，而且很美丽(měilì beautiful)，很有现代感。

1) What is the personality of I. M. Pei like?

2) What are two famous buildings I. M. Pei has designed?

_____

3) Which area of design does he excel in?

_____

4) How do people perceive his works?

_____

Writing

1. Practice writing the following characters in the correct stroke order.

方 方 方 方
面 面 面 面 面 面 面 面 面

方面 | 方面 | 方面 | | |

特 特 特 特 特 特 特 特 特 特
长 长 长 长

特长 | 特长 | 特长 | | |

成 成 成 成 成 成
就 就 就 就 就 就 就 就 就 就 就

成就 | 成就 | 成就 | | |

不 不 不 不
仅 仅 仅 仅

不仁 | 不仁 | 不仁 | | |

2. Who is your favorite movie celebrity? Write the vocabulary that best describes that person's character.

_____
_____

3. Benjamin Franklin was a great man who had many achievements in various fields. List five of them using 在…方面.

_____
_____
_____
_____
_____

4. Write a brief report on five of your classmates' talents, starting with 我的同学们在很多方面都有特长. Write at least two sentences for each classmate.

_____
_____
_____
_____
_____

5. Choose one famous Chinese person, research him/her online and write a brief description of that person, including his or her field, profession, interests and hobbies, achievements, and your opinion of that person. Write at least 250 characters.

LESSON 7 — MAINTAINING A HEALTHY LIFESTYLE

STEP 1 EATING WELL

Listening

1. Listen to the dialog and answer the question.
   QUESTION: Why does Anqi want to drink coke?
   - Ⓐ Coke is tastier than tea.
   - Ⓑ Tea is bitter.
   - Ⓒ Tea is more nutritious than coke.
   - Ⓓ Coke is cheaper.   (   )

2. Listen to the statement and question and choose the most appropriate response.
   - Ⓐ 我妈妈最喜欢喝咖啡。
   - Ⓑ 豆浆很好喝。
   - Ⓒ 我想喝果汁。
   - Ⓓ 我想吃饺子。   (   )

3. Listen to the dialog and answer the question according to the information in the dialog.
   QUESTION: Why do the people in the dialog like vegetables?
   - Ⓐ 蔬菜很好吃。
   - Ⓑ 蔬菜里有铁和钙。
   - Ⓒ 蔬菜里有蛋白质。
   - Ⓓ 蔬菜营养成分高，对健康有好处。   (   )

4. Listen to the dialog and answer the question.
   QUESTION: What is a good reason for eating dairy products?
   - Ⓐ 因为奶制品有很多的蛋白质和钙。
   - Ⓑ 因为豆制品有很多的蛋白质和钙。
   - Ⓒ 因为酸奶很好吃。
   - Ⓓ 因为奶制品对身体好。   (   )

Speaking

1. How do you persuade a person who doesn't like vegetables to eat some vegetables? Use a 吧 sentence and state three reasons.

2. Compare two drinks: tea and coke. Tell which one you prefer and give your reasons. Use the constructions 除了…还… and 虽然…但是… in your answer.

3. What is your favorite dish? How would you recommend it to an exchange student from China? (Say five to eight sentences)

4. What do you eat for breakfast in general? Do you think it is healthy? Why?

Reading

1. Match the food and the nutrition it contains.

   1) 奶制品   A) 蛋白质
   2) 谷物/面包   B) 碳水化合物
   3) 豆制品   C) 脂肪
   4) 海鲜   D) 维生素
   5) 水果   E) 纤维
   6) 蔬菜   F) 钙
   7) 坚果   G) 铁
   8) 肉类   H) 糖

2. Put the Chinese food into the correct categories. (There might be more than one category into which a food item may fall.)

   蛋炒饭，面条，馄饨汤，包子，饺子，春卷，豆腐，酸奶，豆浆，咖啡，果汁，北京烤鸭，炒白菜，蒸鱼，芝麻汤圆，橙子

1) 主食：_____

2) 副食：_____

3) 海鲜：_____

4) 蔬菜：_____

5) 水果：_____

6) 豆制品：_____

7) 奶制品：_____

8) 饮料：_____

9) 甜点：_____

3. Read each sentence and choose an appropriate comment for it.

1) 这个汉堡包有反式脂肪。   (   )

2) 水果有很多维生素，对身体有好处。   (   )

3) 虽然可乐很好喝，但是糖份很高。   (   )

4) 虽然甜点很好吃，但是它糖份也很高。吃多了会胖。   (   )

5) 豆浆除了有蛋白质以外，还有很多铁和钙。   (   )

6) 那种披萨很油，有太多的脂肪，天天吃，对身体不好。   (   )

7) 薯条的卡路里和脂肪都很高。   (   )

A) 很好！多吃一点儿吃吧！
B) 很好！多喝一点儿吃吧！
C) 不太好！少吃一点儿吧！
D) 不太好！少喝一点儿吧！

4. Read the paragraph and answer the questions in Chinese.

> 我弟弟小时候非常喜欢吃甜食。冰淇淋、蛋糕、糖果、巧克力，都是他最爱吃的。每天放学回家，弟弟的第一件事就是打开冰箱拿出一个冰淇淋。妈妈不太喜欢吃甜食，因为她觉得甜食糖份太多，对身体没有好处。所以妈妈常常对弟弟说，少吃一点甜食，多吃点水果吧！但是弟弟觉得水果没有蛋糕和巧克力好吃。后来，弟弟长大了。他在健康课上学到了很多东西，知道了甜食虽然好吃，但是营养成分很少。水果和蔬菜虽然没有那么好吃，但是除了维生素以外，还有很多别的营养成分，所以应该多吃一些。现在弟弟每天吃各种不同的食物，营养很均衡，很健康。

1) 弟弟小时候喜欢吃什么？

_____

2) 弟弟每天放学回到家第一件事是什么？

_____

3) 妈妈也喜欢甜食吗？

_____

4) 弟弟长大以后还吃很多甜食吗？

_____

5) 水果和甜食，哪个比较健康？

_____

Writing

1. Practice writing the following characters in the correct stroke order.

食 食 食 食 食 食 食 食 食
物 物 物 物 物 物 物 物

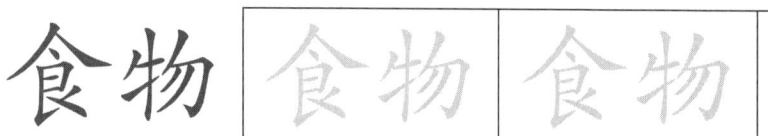

食物　| 食物 | 食物 | | |

营 营 营 营 营 营 营 营 营 营
养 养 养 养 养 养 养 养

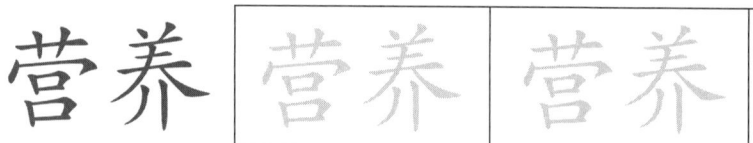

营养　| 营养 | 营养 | | |

健 健 健 健 健 健 健 健 健
康 康 康 康 康 康 康 康 康

健康　| 健康 | 健康 | | |

虽 虽 虽 虽 虽 虽 虽 虽 虽
然 然 然 然 然 然 然 然 然 然 然

虽然　| 虽然 | 虽然 | | |

但但但但但但但
是是是是是是是是是

| 但是 | 但是 | 但是 | | |

2. What food contains the following nutrition? Write one or two examples of each food.

   1) 维生素：_____

   2) 蛋白质：_____

   3) 脂肪：_____

   4) 纤维：_____

   5) 铁：_____

   6) 钙：_____

3. The following foods are commonly served in the U.S. Comment on each of them using 除了…还….

   1) 炸薯条：_____

   2) 蔬菜水果沙拉：_____

   3) 巧克力蛋糕：_____

   4) 可乐：_____

   5) 汉堡包：_____

   6) 披萨：_____

4. What do you like and dislike about Chinese food? What do you like and dislike about Western food? Write two sentences for each of them using 虽然…但是….

   中餐： 1) _____

   2) _____

   西餐： 1) _____

   2) _____

5. Write a short essay on your daily meals. Talk about why you eat these foods, the advantages and disadvantages of these foods in your diet, and how you can improve your diet. (Write at least 250 characters.)

   _____
   _____
   _____
   _____
   _____
   _____
   _____
   _____
   _____
   _____

STEP 2 GETTING SICK

Listening

1. Listen to the dialog and answer the question.
   QUESTION: What symptom does the man not have?
   - Ⓐ 头疼
   - Ⓑ 流鼻涕
   - Ⓒ 发烧
   - Ⓓ 咳嗽   (   )

2. Listen to the dialog and answer the question.
   QUESTION: How many times a day does the woman need to take the medicine?
   - Ⓐ Once
   - Ⓑ Twice
   - Ⓒ Three times
   - Ⓓ Four times   (   )

3. Listen to the dialog and choose the most appropriate response.
   - Ⓐ 我除了发烧，头也很疼。
   - Ⓑ 我的体温(body temperature)很高。
   - Ⓒ 我是打篮球时擦伤的。
   - Ⓓ 我虽然发烧，但是头不疼。   (   )

4. Listen to the statement and question and choose the most appropriate response.
   - Ⓐ 我们现在去医院。
   - Ⓑ 蔬菜非常有营养。
   - Ⓒ 可乐对身体不好。
   - Ⓓ 吃一个冰淇淋吧！   (   )

Speaking

1. Describe the common symptoms of the following illnesses:
   1) a cold
   2) stomach flu

2. Your classmate has vomited, has a stomach ache, and feels sick. Suggest three ways to help him/her feel better.

LESSON 7 MAINTAINING A HEALTHY LIFESTYLE

3. Your Chinese friend has problems understanding the following label regarding the instructions on how to take the medicine. Explain it to him in Chinese.

```
NO 0060023-08291    DATE 05/14/14
JOHN SMITH
123 MAIN STREET ANYTOWN, US 11111
TAKE ONE CAPSULE BY
MOUTH THREE TIMES DAILY
FOR 10 DAYS UNTIL ALL
TAKEN
```

4. Imagine your brother Mike has caught a cold. Inform his teacher for him by leaving a message about his symptoms and ask for the day off. (30 to 45 seconds)

Reading

1. Read the instructions and answer the questions.

   > 药品：维生素B1片
   > 用法用量：一次1片，一天3次。

   1) What is the name of the medicine?

   _____

   2) How often should a patient take the medicine?

   _____

2. Match the problems with the right treatments.

   1) 脚腕扭伤   A) 多喝水，多休息

   2) 感冒头疼   B) 要吃清淡的(qīngdàn)，不要吃油腻的(yóunì)食物
                          light   greasy

   3) 拉肚子   C) 多睡觉，多休息

   4) 消化不良   D) 少做运动，不要用脚

3. Select the most logical response for each of the sentences.

1) 妈妈，我的头很疼，喉咙也疼，还流鼻涕，很不舒服。 (　　)
2) 给你，这是药方(prescription). (　　)
3) 医生，我拉肚子了。 (　　)
4) 这种药，一天吃三次，一次吃两片。饭前吃。不要吃辣的东西。 (　　)

A) 你是不是吃了不干净(gānjìng, clean)的东西了？
B) 谢谢您，医生！请问我一天吃几次，一次吃几片？
C) 你感冒了吧？我带(dài, bring)你去看医生吧？
D) 好！知道了！谢谢你！

4. Read the paragraph and answer the questions in Chinese.

小时候，我胃口不好，不喜欢吃饭，除了甜的食物，什么都不喜欢吃，所以营养不足(bù zú, insufficient)，身体也不好，常常感冒、发烧。爸爸妈妈得常(cháng, often)带我去看医生，很麻烦(máfan, troublesome)。有的时候一个月去看两三次。后来，爸爸妈妈也成了半个医生，一般(yìbān, common)的感冒、着凉(zháoliáng, cold)，他们都知道(zhīdào, know)应该给我吃什么药，一天吃几次，一次吃几片。上小学以后我喜欢上了打篮球，每个星期都要和同学打三、四次篮球。打篮球很累，常常感觉很饿(è, hungry)，慢慢地(mànmàn de, slowly)我的胃口好起来了，也喜欢吃更多不同味道(wèidào, taste)的食物了。这样身体吸收(xīshōu, absorb)了丰富(fēngfù, rich)的营养，越来越(yuè lái yuè, more and more)健康了。现在我很少感冒，几乎(jīhū, almost)一年也不去看一次医生。我觉得运动和饮食(diet)都很重要。我们得保持(bǎochí, maintain)健康的生活习惯(xíguàn, habits)！

1) 我小时候为什么身体不好?
_____

2) 我小时候常常一个月去看几次医生?
_____

3) 后来我的身体为什么越来越好了?
_____

4) 现在我还常常去看病吗?
_____

5) 我觉得什么是健康的生活习惯?
_____

Writing

1. Practice writing the following characters in the correct stroke order.

舒舒舒舒舒舒舒舒舒舒舒
服服服服服服服服

舒服 | 舒服 | 舒服 | | |

生生生生生
病病病病病病病病病病

生病 | 生病 | 生病 | | |

头疼 头头头头头
疼疼疼疼疼疼疼疼疼疼

| 头疼 | 头疼 | | |

感感感感感感感感感感
冒冒冒冒冒冒冒冒冒

感冒

| 感冒 | 感冒 | | |

次次次次次次

次

| 次 | 次 | 次 | | | | | |

片片片片

片

| 片 | 片 | 片 | | | | | |

2. Fill in the blanks to form words on common illnesses.

_____ 疼   _____ 疼

_____ 疼   _____ 疼

_____ 疼   _____ 疼

3. Write down the symptoms you experience when you catch a cold.

___

___

___

4. Answer the questions in full sentences based on your personal life.

1) 你最喜欢的水果是什么？

___

2) 你觉得吃水果健康还是喝可乐健康？为什么？

___

3) 你常常做什么运动？这个运动对你的身体有什么好处？

___

4) 好的饮食习惯对一个人的身体有很多好处。你有什么饮食习惯？

___

5) 你的生活习惯健康吗？有没有你想改进的习惯？

___

5. Describe an experience during which you felt sick. Include details on the time of sickness, the symptoms, and how you got well. (Write at least 100 characters.)

STEP 3 DEVELOPING HEALTHY HABITS

Listening

1. Listen to the question and choose the most appropriate response.
   - Ⓐ 我喜欢玩电脑游戏。
   - Ⓑ 我用电脑做作业。
   - Ⓒ 我用手机(cellphone)上网。
   - Ⓓ 我不能看书。   (   )

2. Listen to the dialog and answer the question.
   QUESTION: Where does this dialog most likely take place?
   - Ⓐ 图书馆
   - Ⓑ 邮局
   - Ⓒ 餐馆
   - Ⓓ 银行   (   )

3. Listen and choose the most logical response.
   - Ⓐ 你应该多吃些健康的食品！
   - Ⓑ 你每天都应该睡最少8个小时的觉，也应该常常运动！
   - Ⓒ 你应该少上网。
   - Ⓓ 你应该多吃水果，少喝可乐。   (   )

4. Listen and choose the most logical response.
   - Ⓐ 你应该每天多喝水。
   - Ⓑ 你应该多吃甜食，就会长胖。
   - Ⓒ 你应该少吃甜食，同时多运动。
   - Ⓓ 吃甜食是一个健康的习惯。   (   )

Speaking

1. What are the products that we use to maintain good daily hygiene? List at least eight of them.

2. Talk about what you can do using the following devices.
   Example:
   笔：我用铅笔写字，也用铅笔画画，还用铅笔玩游戏。
   1) 电脑   2) 手机   3) iPad

3. Your classmate Mary wants to stay fit and healthy. What is your advice on her lifestyle? What should she do and not do? Provide five sentences of what she should do and five sentences of what she should not do.

4. Talk about your involvement with sports. Use the following questions as a guide: What is your favorite sport? How often do you do the sport? How long do you do the sport each time?

Reading

1. Match the items with the right actions.

   1) 沐浴液　　　　A) 梳头
   2) 洗发液　　　　B) 擦鼻涕
   3) 肥皂　　　　　C) 洗澡
   4) 牙膏、牙刷　　D) 洗手
   5) 梳子　　　　　E) 刷牙
   6) 面巾纸　　　　F) 洗头发

2. Fill in the blanks with the appropriate activities.

   A) 洗手　　　B) 洗澡　　　C) 刷牙

   1) 每次吃饭以前，我们应该＿＿＿＿＿＿＿＿＿＿。

   2) 每天睡觉以前，我们应该＿＿＿＿＿＿＿＿＿＿。

   3) 每天早上起床以后，我们应该＿＿＿＿＿＿＿＿＿＿。

   4) 每次运动以后，我们应该＿＿＿＿＿＿＿＿＿＿。

   5) 每次从学校回到家，我们都应该＿＿＿＿＿＿＿＿＿＿。

   6) 每次上卫生间后，我们都应该＿＿＿＿＿＿＿＿＿＿。

3. Read the following habits and check those that you consider healthy.
   1) 早睡早起。   (   )
   2) 晚睡晚起。   (   )
   3) 每周运动四天，每次运动一个小时。   (   )
   4) 每周运动两天，每次运动六个小时。   (   )
   5) 每年做两次体检，半年一次。   (   )
   6) 每天吃一次蔬菜和水果。   (   )
   7) 每天喝很多可乐，吃三次油炸(yóuzhá, fried)食品。 (   )
   8) 每天晚饭后，出去散步半个小时。   (   )

4. Read the email and answer the questions in Chinese.

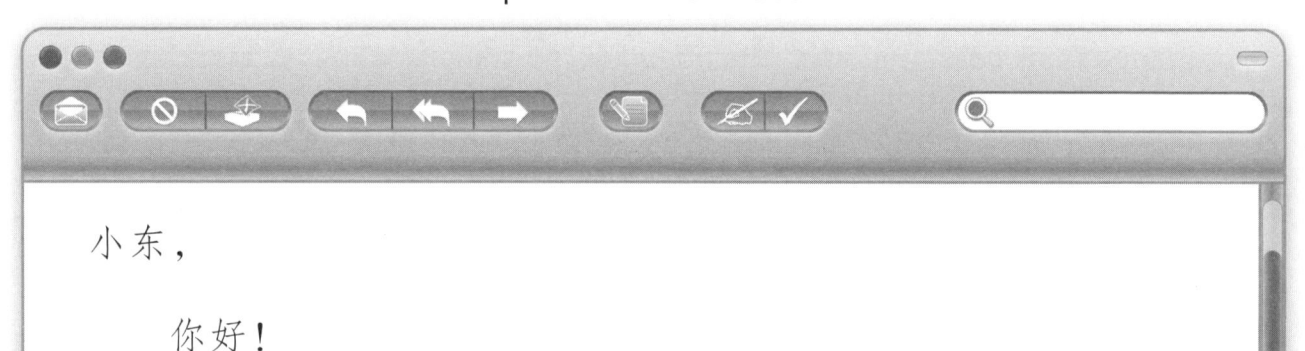

小东，

　　你好！

　　最近过得怎么样？还是跟从前一样忙、一样累吗？

　　我上十年级(jí / grade)了，非常忙。每天最多只能睡七个小时的觉，因为功课很多，所以每天做功课都要用三、四个小时。而且我每天都得运动。在我的学校我们每周运动五天，每天运动两个小时。中国的高中生(high school)也天天运动吗？你们每天运动几个小时？

　　我住在学校里。学校的餐厅给学生提供(tígōng / provide)很丰富、很多样的食物。虽然我们每天都很累、很忙，但是每次走进餐厅我们都非常开心。因为我们有好吃、健康的食物！我们

每天除了主食以外，还有肉、鸡蛋、牛奶、蔬菜和水果。如果你吃素(sùshí vegetarian)，我们每餐还有素食饭菜。我们大家最喜欢的是炸薯条和汉堡包。我觉得虽然不是很健康，但是很好吃。我们每周也只有一天能吃到薯条和汉堡。你在中国一日三餐常常吃什么？你觉得你吃得健康吗？你的生活习惯健康吗？我听说中国人也常吃快餐，中国也有很多麦当劳(Màidāngláo MacDonald's)和肯德基(Kěndéjī Kentucky Fried Chicken)，是真的吗？请给我回信！

　　　　祝你学习进步！

　　　　　　　　　　　小龙
　　　　　　　　　　　十月十五日

1) 小龙的高中生活怎么样？

_____

2) 小龙有什么运动习惯？

_____

3) 小龙喜欢学校餐厅里的食物吗？为什么？

_____

4) 小龙和他的同学最喜欢的食物是什么？你觉得健康吗？

_____

Writing

1. Practice writing the following characters in the correct stroke order.

用 用 用 用 用

用 | 用 | 用 | 用 | | | | |

应 应 应 应 应 应 应
该 该 该 该 该 该 该 该

应该 | 应该 | 应该 | | |

运 运 运 运 运 运 运
动 动 动 动 动 动

运动 | 运动 | 运动 | | |

太 太 太 太

太 | 太 | 太 | 太 | | | | |

分 分 分 分
钟 钟 钟 钟 钟 钟 钟 钟 钟

分钟 | 分钟 | 分钟 | | |

2. What good eating habits do you have? What good habits do you have for staying active? List five habits for each of them.

_____

_____

_____

_____

3. Complete the sentences.

1) 如果你天天吃很多的甜食，_____

2) 如果你每天只睡五个小时，_____

3) 如果你运动过度，_____

4) 虽然茶有一点苦，_____

5) 虽然可乐很好喝，_____

6) 虽然天天运动会有一点累，_____

4. Answer the questions based on your personal life.

1) 你一个星期上几次中文课？一次多少分钟？

_____

2) 你一天打几次电话？一次几分钟？

_____

3) 你一个星期上几次网？一次多长时间？

_____

4) 你一个星期玩几次电脑游戏？一次多长时间？

5) 你一个星期做几次运动？一次多长时间？

5. Write an essay on the topic of staying healthy. You may discuss how one's lifestyle can affect one's health. You may talk about food, sports, work, and rest. Finally, you can also talk about illnesses. Make sure you use 如果…就…，虽然…但是…，最，用, etc. (Write at least 250 characters.)

LESSON 8 CONNECTING WITH OTHERS

STEP 1 USING TECHNOLOGY IN DAILY LIFE

Listening

1. Listen to the dialog and choose the correct response that answers the question.
   QUESTION: 马克的新数码相机怎么样？
   Ⓐ 好用，但是很大。　　　Ⓑ 好用、美观。
   Ⓒ 轻巧、功能多。　　　　Ⓓ 美观、功能多。　　　　（　　）

2. Listen to the statement and choose the most logical response.
   Ⓐ 你的打印机既实用又轻巧。
   Ⓑ 你买一台新的吧。
   Ⓒ 我哥哥会修理数码相机。
   Ⓓ 我要买一台新的打印机。　　　　（　　）

3. Listen to the statement and choose the most logical response.
   Ⓐ 我的电脑坏了。
   Ⓑ 我不知道。我们今天上不了网了吧？
   Ⓒ 我们今天的功课很多。
   Ⓓ 网上的新闻很多。　　　　（　　）

4. Listen to the statement and answer the question.
   QUESTION: Why did he buy a new computer?
   Ⓐ He did not like the old computer.
   Ⓑ The new computer has more functions.
   Ⓒ The old computer was broken.
   Ⓓ There was a discount for a new computer.　　　　（　　）

Speaking

1. What IT (information technology) products do you have at home? What advantages have they brought you?

2. What IT products do you use in your classroom? What advantages have they brought you?

3. What is your favorite IT product? Why do you like it?

4. Imagine you encounter some problems with your laptop computer. Work with a partner and create a dialog on how you would contact technical support and make an appointment for repair.

Reading

1. Choose the word that best describes each of the following products.

功能多　耐用　快速　美观　轻巧　实用

1) 打印机 _____
2) 电脑 _____
3) 数码相机 _____
4) 手机 _____
5) 冰箱 _____

2. How can you use the following products? Match each product with an appropriate function.

1) 电脑　　　　　　　　　A) 打印作业
2) 打印机　　　　　　　　B) 上网找资料
3) 手机　　　　　　　　　C) 拍照 (pāizhào, take photos)
4) 冰箱　　　　　　　　　D) 上网看电影
5) 数码相机　　　　　　　E) 保存 (bǎocún, store) 食物
6) 平板电脑　　　　　　　F) 打电话

STEP UP WITH CHINESE 2

3. From the statements below, choose the most appropriate option to complete each sentence.

1) _____，我可以打印了。

2) _____，我们可以拍照了。

3) _____，我现在上得了网了。

4) _____，我上不了网。

5) _____，我打不了电话。

A) 我的电脑坏了
B) 我买了数码相机
C) 我的打印机修好了
D) 我的网络安装好了
E) 我的手机丢(diū, lost)了

4. Read the paragraph and answer the questions in Chinese.

平板电脑和笔记本电脑都是很好的IT产品(chǎnpǐn)。和传统(chuántǒng)的电脑相比(xiāngbǐ)，它们都很轻巧，而且功能很多。平板电脑比手机大，比笔记本(bǐjìběn, notebook)电脑小。平板电脑有很大的显示屏，所以如果你想看电影或者(huòzhě)电子(electronic)书，用平板电脑最好。笔记本电脑没有平板电脑那么轻巧，但是它的功能比平板电脑要多得多。还有笔记本电脑的键盘比较大，如果你需要(xūyào, need)打(type)很多的字，用笔记本电脑更方便。因为平板电脑和笔记本电脑都可以上网，所以都有可能

> gǎnrǎn　　　　　yīncǐ　shǐyòng　　　　　　　　　suíbiàn　　　　bù shúxī
> 感染病毒。因此使用的时候都要小心，不要随便安装不熟悉
> infected with　　therefore　use　　　　　careful　　　careless　　　unfamiliar
> 　　　　　lìngwài　　　　　　　　　　　　　　jīngmì
> 的软件。另外笔记本电脑和平板电脑都是精密的电子产品，
> 　　　　in addition　　　　　　　　　　　　sophisticated
> 　　　　　　　　　yídìng　　zhuānyè rényuán
> 如果出了问题，一定要请专业人员来修理，不能自己随便
> 　　　　　　　　must　　　professional personnel
> chāzhuāng
> 拆装。
> dismantle and assemble

1) What are two similarities between a tablet computer and a notebook computer?

_____

2) What are two differences between a tablet computer and a notebook computer?

_____

3) If you want to watch a movie, which product would you use?

_____

4) If you need to type an essay, which product would you use?

_____

5) How do we prevent computers from getting infected with a virus?

_____

6) What should you do if you have problems with a tablet or a notebook computer?

_____

Writing

1. Practice writing the following characters in the correct stroke order.

轻轻轻轻轻轻轻轻轻
巧巧巧巧巧

轻巧

耐耐耐耐耐耐耐耐耐
用用用用用

耐用

坏坏坏坏坏坏坏

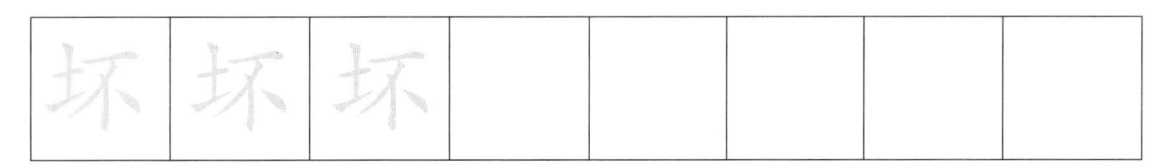

坏

修修修修修修修修
理理理理理理理理理

修理

安安安安安安
装装装装装装装装装装装

安装

问题 问题 问题

2. Complete the sentences by writing what you can't do in the following situations.

  Example: 打印机坏了，<u>所以现在打印不了文件</u>。

  1) 数码相机坏了，_____。

  2) 电脑坏了，_____。

  3) 手机坏了，_____。

  4) 电脑的显示屏坏了，_____。

  5) 车坏了，_____。

3. Provide reasons for the following statements using 既…又….

  1) 我喜欢带(dài, bring)平板电脑出门，不带电脑，因为

  _____。

  2) 现在人们喜欢用数码相机，不用传统相机，因为

  _____。

  3) 人们喜欢坐飞机旅行，不会自己开车，因为

  _____。

4. What is your favorite IT product? Write about it by describing its functions, its advantages, and how your life would be without it. (Write at least 250 characters.)

STEP 2 COMMUNICATING WITH OTHERS

Listening

1. Listen and choose the most logical response to the question.
   - Ⓐ 我喜欢QQ。
   - Ⓑ 我的朋友在中国。
   - Ⓒ 我在美国有很多朋友。
   - Ⓓ 我们用脸书、推特跟朋友聊天。   (   )

2. Listen and choose the most logical response to the question.
   - Ⓐ 我弟弟和你弟弟是好朋友。
   - Ⓑ 你应该和弟弟一起玩游戏。
   - Ⓒ 你弟弟不应该花太多时间上网。
   - Ⓓ 我弟弟不喜欢电脑，他喜欢运动。   (   )

3. Listen to the dialog and answer the question.
   QUESTION: How does Anqi keep in touch with her family in China?
   - Ⓐ 她给家人打电话。   Ⓑ 她给家人发电邮。
   - Ⓒ 她用网络视频电话。   Ⓓ 她不常和家人联系。   (   )

4. Listen to the dialog and answer the question.
   QUESTION: How does Fangfang keep in touch with her friend Sally?
   - Ⓐ 看电影   Ⓑ 打网球
   - Ⓒ 打电话   Ⓓ 用脸书   (   )

5. Listen to the dialog and answer the question.
   QUESTION: Which statement correctly describes both their younger brothers?
   - Ⓐ 他们都喜欢看电视。
   - Ⓑ 他们都喜欢上网。
   - Ⓒ 他们都喜欢打球。
   - Ⓓ 他们都喜欢写博客。   (   )

Speaking

1. What are the popular social websites you often use? What do you use them for? Give two examples.

2. Talk about the activities you do with others at the following times.
   Example: 7:30am   我和弟弟一起上学。

   7:30am   8:30am   12:00pm   3:00pm   6:00pm   8:00pm

3. Talk about your hobbies. What are they? How often do you do these things and with whom?

4. Research online to find out more about the following people. Select one and give a brief description including his hobbies, key achievements, as well as what people can do using their products.

   Mark Zuckerberg; Jack Dorsey; Steve Chen; Yun Ma; Huateng Ma

Reading

1. Match the popular websites with their functions.

   1) 脸书   A) 看免费视频、电影、电视。
                         (miǎnfèi = free)

   2) 推特   B) 写你的心情，写文章。
                         (xīnqíng = feelings, wénzhāng = essay)

   3) 博客   C) 分享你的照片，看朋友的照片。

   4) YouTube   D) 和朋友联系，和他们分享你的生活。
                         (shēnghuó = life)

   5) Flickr   E) 时时了解对你重要的人(事情)。
                         (shíshí = constantly, liǎojiě = know, zhòngyào = important, shìqing = event)

LESSON 8 CONNECTING WITH OTHERS

2. Match the following software and utilities with their functions.

   1) iTunes　　　　　A) 搜索资料
   2) Angry birds　　B) 发电邮
   3) Skype　　　　　C) 写博客
   4) Outlook　　　　D) 打电话、视频聊天
   5) Blogger　　　　E) 玩游戏
   6) Google　　　　 F) 下载歌曲

3. Read the following signs of popular websites in China. Choose five of them and find out what they are. Then write one sentence to describe each of them.

_____

_____

_____

_____

4. Read the paragraph and choose the correct response to answer the questions.

今天人们的生活中少不了电脑和互联网(hùliánwǎng/Internet)。我们用电脑工作、学习、娱乐(yúlè/entertain)，还有和家人、朋友联系。我们可以用电脑上互联网，在网上订餐(dìngcān/order food)、学中文、购物、交朋友(make friends)、看电影、写博客、搜集资料、玩游戏和发电邮。电脑和互联网让(ràng/let)我们的生活更加(gèngjiā/more)方便、有趣(yǒuqù/interesting)，但是有时候它们也让人花太多时间。很多年轻人每天都用很多时间在网上看新闻、聊天、玩电脑游戏。但他们和身边的人交流的时间却很少。所以如果你喜欢上网，要注意(zhùyì/mindful)不要在网上花太多时间。

1) Which online activity is not mentioned in the paragraph?
   Ⓐ 和家人联系　　　Ⓑ 买东西
   Ⓒ 玩电脑游戏　　　Ⓓ 下载歌曲　　　　　　　　(　　)

2) What is the advantage of using a computer and the Internet?
   Ⓐ 健康、快乐　　　Ⓑ 方便、有趣
   Ⓒ 轻巧、实用　　　Ⓓ 美观、耐用　　　　　　　　(　　)

3) Which statement is clearly mentioned in the paragraph?
   Ⓐ 不要上网看新闻　　　Ⓑ 不要上网搜索信息
   Ⓒ 不要在网上花太多时间　　Ⓓ 不要在网上购物　(　　)

Writing

1. Practice writing the following characters in the correct stroke order.

朋 朋 朋 朋 朋 朋 朋 朋
友 友 友 友

朋友 | 朋友 | 朋友 | | |

联 联 联 联 联 联 联 联 联 联 联 联
系 系 系 系 系 系 系

联系 | 联系 | 联系 | | |

分 分 分 分
享 享 享 享 享 享 享 享

分享 | 分享 | 分享 | | |

购 购 购 购 购 购 购 购
物 物 物 物 物 物 物 物

购物 | 购物 | 购物 | | |

下 下 下
载 载 载 载 载 载 载 载 载

下载 | 下载 | 下载 | | |

164

STEP UP WITH CHINESE 2

2. What can you do using the Internet? List at least 10 things you can do.

___

3. The following chart shows the activities each student does on Saturday mornings. Write a sentence about each using 不是…就是….

   Example: 我　　购物　　电影　　　我星期六不是购物，就是看电影。

Tom	跑步	打篮球	_____
Lily	看书	做功课	_____
Mike	上网	看电影	_____
Kate	画画	弹钢琴	_____
Mary	游泳	爬山	_____

4. Write one sentence on how you use each of the following utilities: Twitter, Flickr, Skype, Blogger, Wikipedia, Google, YouTube, and Microsoft Outlook.

   Example: 我用Facebook和朋友联系。

___

LESSON 8 CONNECTING WITH OTHERS

STEP 3 GATHERING INFORMATION

Listening

1. Listen to the statement and choose the most logical response.
   - Ⓐ 中文很难但是我觉得很有用。
   - Ⓑ 我最喜欢星期一的课。
   - Ⓒ 真的吗？这个消息你是从哪儿听来的？
   - Ⓓ 星期二我们没有中文课。 ( )

2. Listen and choose the most logical response.
   - Ⓐ 这太浪费(waste)时间了。
   - Ⓑ 他非常聪明。
   - Ⓒ 他家人在美国吗？
   - Ⓓ 你朋友是哪国人？ ( )

3. Listen to the dialog and choose the response that most logically answers the question.
   QUESTION: What does the woman's Saturday morning look like?
   - Ⓐ 早起，游泳
   - Ⓑ 晚起，跑步
   - Ⓒ 早起，跑步
   - Ⓓ 晚起，吃早饭 ( )

4. Listen to the dialog and answer the question.
   QUESTION: What is the woman's preferred source for news?
   - Ⓐ 电视
   - Ⓑ 网络
   - Ⓒ 报纸
   - Ⓓ 广播 ( )

Speaking

1. What are the media you often use to get news?

2. What is your favorite leisure activity? Talk about the time that you always do the activity using 一…就….

3. Talk about five things that will happen once you go online using 只要…就….

4. Search for some interesting news, and choose one piece of news to share with your classmates. Make sure you include the news source.

Reading

1. Match the Chinese media with their translations.

   1) 中国新闻网   A) Sina
   2) 新浪网   B) China Daily
   3) 中国日报   C) Beijing Morning News
   4) 北京早报   D) Beijing Transportation Broadcasting Station
   5) 北京晚报   E) Central People's Broadcasting Station
   6) 中国中央电视台   F) China Central Television
   7) 中央人民广播电台   G) China News Service
   8) 北京交通广播电台   H) Beijing Evening News

2. Read the sentences and determine whether they are true (T) or false (F) according to the pictures.

   1) 这条新闻我是从网上看到的。   (   )

   2) 这首歌他是从网上听到的。   (   )

LESSON 8 CONNECTING WITH OTHERS

3) 我看了电视新闻才知道这个消息。　　（　　）

4) 他一上网就读到这条新闻了。　　（　　）

5) 她一看广告就获得这个信息了。　　（　　）

3. Match the questions with the right answers.

1) 你的中文书是从哪儿买的？
2) 这周第一节中文课是从几点到几点？
3) 这条新闻你是从哪儿看到的？
4) 这首歌你是从哪儿听到的？
5) 这条信息是谁发给你的？

A) 妈妈
B) 朋友的iPod里
C) 八点到八点四十五分
D) 北京
E) 纽约时报

4. Read the following news report and answer the questions in Chinese.

> 6月25日，北京大学中文夏令营开营的第一天，迎来了来自全球十五个国家的中文留学生。学生们将在6月25日到7月25日的一个月的时间里学习中国文化和中文。每年夏天北京大学都会举办这个中文夏令营。
>
> quánqiú — worldwide
> liúxuéshēng — overseas student
> jǔbàn — hold
>
> 中国新闻网北京
> 6月25日　王小明
> 十月十五日

1) What is the source of this news item?

_____

2) Who is the journalist?

_____

3) Where is the summer camp?

_____

4) What will the students learn in this camp?

_____

Writing

1. Practice writing the following characters in the correct stroke order.

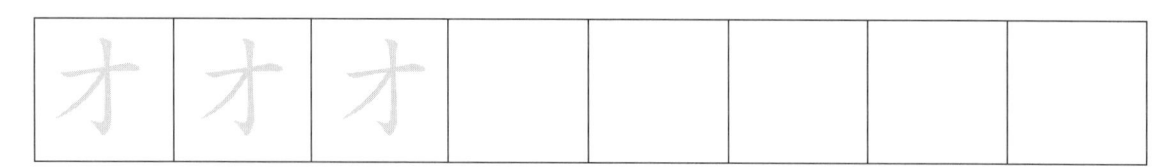

才 才 才

才

知知知知知知知知
道道道道道道道道道道道

知道

听听听听听听听

听

消消消消消消消消消
息息息息息息息息

消息

新新新新新新新新新新
闻闻闻闻闻闻闻闻

新闻

查 查查查查查查查查查

找 找找找找找找找

2. Fill in the blanks with 就 or 才.

1) 我昨天晚上八点（　　　）睡觉了。我的室友十一点（　　　）睡觉。

2) 同学们前天（　　　）知道了这个消息。我今天下午（　　　）知道。

3) 这条新闻报纸上今天（　　　）有，网上几天前（　　　）有了。

4) 北京的天气冷得早，九月底（　　　）凉下来了。上海冷得很晚，常常到了十月底（　　　）开始凉下来。

5) 他是一个很有精力的人，每天晚上十一点（　　　）睡觉，第二天早上五点（　　　）起床。

3. Complete the sentences.

   Example: 今天小明一起床，就去体育馆运动。

   1) 每天早上王芳芳一吃完早饭，_____。

   2) 妈妈每天一下班，_____。

   3) 她一考完试，_____。

   4) 夏天我们一有时间，_____。

   5) 李文一上网，_____。

4. Provide appropriate conditions in the first part of the sentences to match the results in the second part of the sentences.

   Example: 只要明天不下雨，我就去踢足球。

   1) _____，他就上网看电影。

   2) _____，她就点酸辣汤。

   3) _____，她就会带着(dài / bring)她的小狗出去散步。

   4) _____，你就会看到墙上的照片。

   5) _____，你就会看到这条新闻。

5. How do you and your family members acquire news and other useful information? Do you read the newspaper, listen to the radio, watch TV, or get news and information from the Internet? Write a paragraph talking about the media today and describe how members of your family use media. (200 characters)

LESSON 9 — GETTING ALONG WITH OTHERS

STEP 1 HELPING AT HOME

Listening

1. Listen to the statement and question and choose the most logical response.
   - Ⓐ 我每天都遛狗。
   - Ⓑ 我没去过中国。
   - Ⓒ 好，我也有一只狗，我就一起喂。
   - Ⓓ 我的狗吃得很多。   (   )

2. Listen to the statement and question and choose the most logical response.
   - Ⓐ 我也会帮忙。   Ⓑ 我爸爸妈妈每天做家务。
   - Ⓒ 我家人很喜欢做家务。   Ⓓ 我的功课很多。   (   )

3. Listen to the dialog and answer the question.
   QUESTION: Why does the woman offer to help the man?
   - Ⓐ 他感冒了。   Ⓑ 他不知道餐厅在哪儿。
   - Ⓒ 他的脚不能走路。   Ⓓ 他喜欢别人帮忙。   (   )

4. Listen to the dialog and answer the question.
   QUESTION: What does Fangfang offer to do? (Check all that apply.)
   - Ⓐ 浇花   (   )
   - Ⓑ 擦桌子   (   )
   - Ⓒ 洗厕所   (   )
   - Ⓓ 吸尘   (   )
   - Ⓔ 洗碗   (   )
   - Ⓕ 遛狗   (   )
   - Ⓖ 倒垃圾   (   )

Speaking

1. What are the household chores you are able to do yourself? Give at least eight examples.

2. Your neighbors are going on a vacation without their pet cats. Tell how you can help them.

3. How are household chores shared among your family members?

4. What are the things that you will help with if you have time?
   Example: 要是我有空的话，我就帮弟弟温习功课。

Reading

1. How would you divide the following work among four family members, so that everyone shares a reasonable proportion of the chores? Match the household chores to the family members.

   A) 洗碗
   B) 倒垃圾
   C) 叠衣服
   D) 整理房间
   E) 摆碗筷
   F) 做饭
   G) 割草
   H) 洗车
   I) 喂狗
   J) 遛狗
   K) 浇花
   L) 吸尘

   1) 爸爸（四十五岁）
   2) 妈妈（四十三岁）
   3) 姐姐（十六岁）
   4) 弟弟（十二岁）

2. Fill in the blanks with the options provided below.

我弟弟很热心(rèxīn/earnest)，很喜欢帮助人。要是我们的邻居需要有人帮忙看小孩，他总是说(zǒngshì shuō/always say)，"我来吧！"在家里他也常常(chángcháng/often)帮爸爸（　　　），帮妈妈（　　　）。他还想帮爸爸（　　　），但是爸爸觉得这有点危险(wēixiǎn/dangerous)，所以爸爸总是自己(zìjǐ/oneself)做。弟弟的爱好很多，他喜欢音乐、体育，也喜欢种花，养(yǎng/keep, raise)宠物。要是他有时间的话，他就会（　　　）、（　　　）、（　　　）。

- Ⓐ 洗车
- Ⓑ 喂狗
- Ⓒ 遛狗
- Ⓓ 浇花
- Ⓔ 吸尘
- Ⓕ 割草

3. Match the question with the most logical answer.

1) 明天下午你有空吗？　　　　　　　　　　　　　　　（　　）
2) 夏天草长得很快，我每个星期都得帮爸爸割草，你呢？（　　）
3) 你觉得吸尘容易还是扫地容易？　　　　　　　　　　（　　）
4) 要是你有时间，你会帮忙做家务吗？　　　　　　　　（　　）
5) 我们家的邻居要出去旅游，他们请我帮忙喂狗。你觉得我可以帮忙吗？　　　　　　　　　　　　　　　　　　　　（　　）

A) 我爸爸不让(ràng/allow)我割草，他自己割草，他说割草机(lawn mower)太大，我不能用。

B) 当然可以！你自己不是也有一只狗吗？一起喂吧。

C) 没空，我得帮妈妈打扫房子、浇花、割草。

D) 我的功课太多了，不会有太多时间做家务。

E) 我觉得吸尘比较容易。虽然有点吵，但是很干净。

4. Read the paragraph and answer the questions.

> 在中国，孩子们在家里常常帮父母做家务。女孩子常常会洗碗、叠衣服、整理房间、扫地、擦桌子等等。男孩子常常会帮忙倒垃圾、拖地板等等。在美国，孩子们也会帮爸爸妈妈做事情。吸尘、洗车、割草、喂狗、遛狗都是常见(chángjiàn / common)的家务。有些美国孩子还会帮助邻居做事，赚(zhuàn / earn)些零用钱(língyòngqián / pocket money)。在中国，大人一般(yìbān / adults normally)不会付(fù / pay)钱请小孩子帮忙做家务，因为他们觉得小孩子帮大人的忙是应该的。

1) 在中国，女孩子常常帮父母做什么家务？

_____

2) 在中国，男孩子常常帮父母做什么家务？

_____

3) 在美国，有哪些常见的家务工作？

_____

4) 美国孩子帮别人(biéren / others)做家务会有什么收获(shōuhuò / benefit)？

_____

5) 在中国，孩子帮大人做家务，大人会不会给小孩子钱？

_____

Writing

1. Practice writing the following characters in the correct stroke order.

帮助

家务

整理

擦

浇

有空　有空　有空

2. Write 10 household chores that you do in your home or that you could do if you had enough time.

_____
_____
_____

3. Complete the sentences using 可以 to offer help.

1) 要是你出门的话，_____。

2) 要是我明天有时间，_____。

3) 要是明天不下雨，_____。

4) 要是你觉得数学很难，_____。

5) 要是你们要去看电影，_____。

6) 要是你做饭的话，_____。

4. What are the things that you can help others with from Monday to Sunday? Write something for each day.

星期一：我帮老师擦白板。

星期二：_____。

179

LESSON 9 GETTING ALONG WITH OTHERS

星期三：_____。

星期四：_____。

星期五：_____。

星期六：_____。

星期日：_____。

5. Write a journal on a day of housework in the format of a diary. The beginning is provided as follows. (Write at least 200 characters.)

五月十七号　　　　星期六　　　　晴
今天我在家里帮妈妈做了一天的家务。

STEP 2 BEING A GOOD NEIGHBOR

Listening

1. Listen and choose the most logical response.
   - Ⓐ 我喜欢你的包。
   - Ⓑ 你的包在哪里?
   - Ⓒ 当然可以。
   - Ⓓ 我不知道。   (　　)

2. Listen and choose the most logical response.
   - Ⓐ 吸尘太吵了。
   - Ⓑ 我不喜欢吸尘。
   - Ⓒ 你周末要去看电影吗?
   - Ⓓ 太好了！我周末要去买菜，还要洗衣服，没时间吸尘。   (　　)

3. Listen to the dialog and answer the question.
   QUESTION: What does Mark want to do on Saturday?
   - Ⓐ 打球
   - Ⓑ 打扫房间
   - Ⓒ 浇花
   - Ⓓ 洗衣服   (　　)

4. Listen to the dialog and answer the question.
   QUESTION: What is the woman's request?
   - Ⓐ To buy a sandwich for her.
   - Ⓑ To buy a can of coke for her.
   - Ⓒ To wash the dishes for her.
   - Ⓓ To walk the dog for her.   (　　)

Speaking

1. How do you ask for help when you have problems with your homework?

2. How do you ask a family member to help you with the household chores?

3. When you see a person getting lost in town, how do you offer help? What would you say to this person?

4. When your neighbor is away from home, how would you offer to help walk the dog?

Reading

1. On the first day of the new school year, there are volunteers helping new students. These words are written on the volunteers' shirts: 我可以帮助您吗？ What do they mean?

2. Read the note and choose the task that the writer would like Mary to do.

   > 亲爱的玛丽，
   >
   > 我妈妈生病了。我这个周末（星期六和星期日）得在医院照顾(zhàogù take care of)妈妈。我的狗不能跟我一起去医院。你有时间帮我喂狗和遛狗吗？一天要喂三次，遛两次。
   >
   > 请给我打手机(135 1100 5468)。
   >
   > 谢谢你的帮助！
   >
   > 小新

   Ⓐ 去医院　　　　　　　　Ⓑ 遛狗和喂狗
   Ⓒ 给小新打电话　　　　　Ⓓ 看小新的妈妈　　　　　　(　　)

3. Match the question or statement with the most appropriate response.

   1) 你需要帮助吗？ (　　)
   2) 你可以帮我一个忙吗？ (　　)
   3) 要是你有时间，可以教我数学吗？ (　　)
   4) 请你帮我把书还(huán return)到图书馆，可以吗？ (　　)
   5) 让我帮你学中文吧！ (　　)

   A) 行，没问题，我也打算去还书。
   B) 当然可以！是什么忙？

C) 太谢谢你了！我的中文很差(chā/bad)。

D) 不用了，谢谢你！

E) 对不起，我今天没有时间。

4. Read the dialog and determine whether the following statements are true (T) or false (F).

> 妈妈：搬家真(zhēn/really)是麻烦！有太多的东西要整理。
>
> 小明：没关系(méi guànxi/don't worry)，我有时间可以帮忙！
>
> 妈妈：太好了！你先帮我把书都放到纸箱(zhǐxiāng/carton)里，然后把衣服都放到衣箱(yīxiāng/clothing box)里，再把纸箱和衣箱都搬到客厅里。
>
> 小明：没问题！妈妈，要不要先把垃圾倒了，把衣服都洗好了？
>
> 妈妈：对！那你先帮忙倒垃圾、洗衣服吧。然后再把衣服和书装到箱子里。有你帮忙太好了！

1) 小明要搬家。 (　　)
2) 小明很忙，没有时间帮忙。 (　　)
3) 小明的妈妈要小明帮忙整理书和衣服。 (　　)
4) 小明会先把垃圾倒了，把衣服洗了。 (　　)
5) 小明会先把书和衣服装到箱子里。 (　　)

Writing

1. Practice writing the following characters in the correct stroke order.

需需需需需需需需需需需需需
要要要要要要要要要

需要 | 需要 | 需要 | | |

当当当当当当
然然然然然然然然然然然

当然 | 当然 | 当然 | | |

让让让让让让

让 | 让 | 让 | 让 | | | | |

干干干
净净净净净净净净

干净 | 干净 | 干净 | | |

完完完完完完完

完 | 完 | 完 | 完 | | | | |

打 打 打 打 打
扫 扫 扫 扫 扫 扫

打扫 | 打扫 | 打扫 | | |

2. Complete the following 把 - sentences.

   1) 我帮爸爸把草 _____。

   2) 爸爸帮我把功课做 _____。

   3) 我帮妈妈把垃圾 _____。

   4) 姐姐帮妈妈把碗 _____。

   5) 哥哥帮妈妈把地板 _____。

   6) 我帮爸爸把车 _____。

   7) 他帮妈妈把厕所 _____。

   8) 他帮邻居把狗 _____。

3. Write a sentence offering help for each of the following situations.

   1) a lady trying to put big luggage in the overhead bin on a plane

   _____

   2) a blind person trying to cross the street

   _____

LESSON 9 GETTING ALONG WITH OTHERS

3) a little boy trying to reach a book on a shelf

_____

4) a man carrying a big box while trying to open the door

_____

5) a group of children trying to reach their ball in a tree

_____

4. Write a sentence seeking help for each of the following situations.

1) You need to go for a meeting, leaving a young child by himself.

_____

2) You do not know the English homework for today.

_____

3) You do not know how to write an email using an iPad.

_____

4) Your room is messy. You are tied up with other work and cannot clean it.

_____

5) You need to return a book to your math teacher, but you don't have the time.

_____

5. Imagine tomorrow is Mother's Day/Father's Day. Write an email to your mom/dad talking about her/his hard work at home and offering your help with the household chores this weekend. (Write at least 200 characters.)

STEP 3 WORKING WITH OTHERS

Listening

1. Listen to the telephone message and choose the most logical response.
   - Ⓐ 数学太难了。
   - Ⓑ 我的数学学得不太好。
   - Ⓒ 好，没问题！
   - Ⓓ 明天我没有数学课。 ( )

2. Listen to the statement and choose the most logical response.
   - Ⓐ 他真是喜欢手机。
   - Ⓑ 他不应该这样(like this)，太危险(dangerous)了。
   - Ⓒ 我哥哥喜欢上网。
   - Ⓓ 我不喜欢开车。 ( )

3. Listen to the dialog and answer the question.
   QUESTION: What does the man mean by his answer?
   - Ⓐ 孩子应该帮忙做家务。
   - Ⓑ 他不同意女生的看法。
   - Ⓒ 他的孩子会帮忙做家务。
   - Ⓓ 他觉得女孩子应该帮忙做家务。 ( )

4. Listen to the dialog and answer the question.
   QUESTION: What does the man mean by his answer?
   - Ⓐ 他们的中文功课多。
   - Ⓑ 虽然他们功课多，但是他们还是应该做这些功课。
   - Ⓒ 他们的中文功课不太多。
   - Ⓓ 他们的中文学得不好。 ( )

Speaking

1. Do you often do two things at the same time? Give five examples using 一边…一边….

2. Someone has suggested that we ban the Internet for high school students to prevent time wasted on it. What is your view on this idea? Do you agree with this suggestion? Why or why not?

3. Many people believe that Chinese is easy to learn. Do you agree or not? Why?

4. Your friend plans to travel to Paris for the weekend. You don't think it is a good idea. How would you advise him or her against doing it?

Reading

1. Choose the option that has the same meaning as the sentence.

   1) 我不是不同意。 (　　)
      - Ⓐ 我同意。
      - Ⓑ 我不同意。

   2) 我不是不喜欢这里。 (　　)
      - Ⓐ 我喜欢这里。
      - Ⓑ 我不喜欢这里。

   3) 这个公园漂亮是漂亮。 (　　)
      - Ⓐ 这个公园不漂亮。
      - Ⓑ 这个公园很漂亮。

2. Write a check for those statements that you agree with and a cross for those you do not agree with.

   1) 你不可以一边走路，一边看书。 (　　)
   2) 你可以一边看电视，一边做功课。 (　　)
   3) 你可以一边发短信，一边过马路。 (　　)
   4) 你不可以一边打电话，一边开车。 (　　)
   5) 你可以一边做功课，一边听音乐。 (　　)

3. Read the paragraph and answer the questions.

> 现在越来越多的人用电脑和手机。人们常常忙着看自己的短信和网上的新闻，忘了关心身边的人和事。我觉得这是不对的。我们应该多关心我们的家人、朋友和社会，而不是网络世界中的人和事。你同意我的看法吗？
>
> yuè lái yuè duō — more and more
> wàng — forget; guānxīn — care for; shì — matter
> shèhuì — society

1) True or false: The author believes the people in the real world are more important than those in the cyber world. (　　)

2) If you agree with the author and are asked to write a reply, which sentence can be used as the first sentence in your reply? (Check all that apply.)
   - Ⓐ 我觉得你说得很有道理。(　　)
   - Ⓑ 我喜欢你的建议。(　　)
   - Ⓒ 我不同意你的看法。(　　)
   - Ⓓ 我的想法和你的一样。(　　)

3) If you disagree and are asked to write a reply, which sentence can you use as the first sentence in your reply? (Check all that apply.)
   - Ⓐ 我觉得你说得没有道理。(　　)
   - Ⓑ 我不同意你的看法。(　　)
   - Ⓒ 我不需要你的帮忙。(　　)
   - Ⓓ 我的想法和你的不太一样。(　　)

Writing

1. Practice writing the following characters in the correct stroke order.

同 同 同 同 同 同
意 意 意 意 意 意 意 意 意 意 意

同意 | 同意 | 同意 | | |

看 看 看 看 看 看 看 看 看
法 法 法 法 法 法 法 法

看法 | 看法 | 看法 | | |

认 认 认 认
为 为 为 为

认为 | 认为 | 认为 | | |

说 说 说 说 说 说 说 说 说

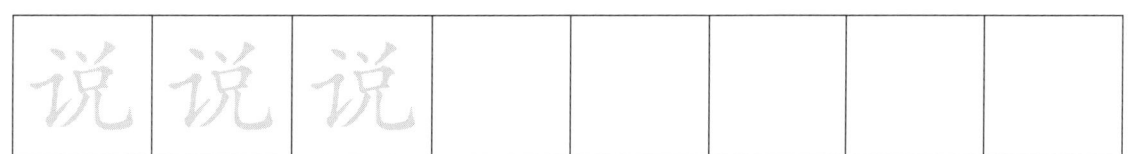

说 | 说 | 说 | 说 | | | | | |

建 建 建 建 建 建 建 建
议 议 议 议 议

建议 | 建议 | 建议 | | |

LESSON 9 GETTING ALONG WITH OTHERS

2. Write three different responses to this statement: 我觉得运动对健康有好处。

   1) _____。

   2) _____。

   3) _____。

3. Write a sentence to state your disagreement with each of the following statements using the construction "adjective + 是 + adjective, 可是…."

   Example: 坐飞机旅行很快。→ 坐飞机快是快，可是不太方便。

   1) 快餐好吃极了。_____

   2) 用手机上网很方便。_____

   3) 暑假呆在家里很安全(ānquán/safe)。_____

   4) 那家书店离这里很远。_____

   5) 住在家里比住在学校舒服。_____

4. What are the things that people like to do at the same time? What are the things that should not be done at the same time? Write three sentences for each.

   Example: 人们喜欢一边吃饭，一边看电视。
   你不可以一边吃饭，一边唱歌。

   _____
   _____
   _____
   _____

5. Write a note to your friend who plans to spend the weekend watching movies. Give your thoughts on how to spend the weekend and your suggestions. (Write at least 200 characters.)

> 小李，
>   你好！
>   我听说你要花两天的周末时间看电影。

LESSON 10 BEING A GLOBAL CITIZEN

STEP 1 BEING PART OF A COMMUNITY

Listening

1. Listen and choose the most appropriate response.
   - Ⓐ 我的爸爸妈妈都是音乐家。
   - Ⓑ 我的爸爸妈妈都喜欢音乐。
   - Ⓒ 爸爸妈妈对哥哥的中文学习有很大影响。
   - Ⓓ 我将来想当律师，因为我的爸爸妈妈都是律师。   (   )

2. Listen and choose the most appropriate response.
   - Ⓐ 她学习很努力，每天很早起床，很晚才睡觉。
   - Ⓑ 她有礼貌又大方。我觉得她人很好，也容易相处。
   - Ⓒ 她不但聪明而且很友善。
   - Ⓓ 她喜欢运动，每天去公园跑步。   (   )

3. Listen to the dialog and answer the question.
   QUESTION: Why does the woman agree with the man?
   - Ⓐ 因为她的中文老师对她有很大影响。
   - Ⓑ 因为她喜欢看报纸。
   - Ⓒ 因为她受她的英文老师的影响很大，也喜欢看新闻。
   - Ⓓ 因为她不喜欢看电视。   (   )

4. Listen to the dialog and answer the question.
   QUESTION: What is Xiaoming like?
   - Ⓐ 爱管闲事，很多人都不喜欢帮他。
   - Ⓑ 开朗，热心，性格好
   - Ⓒ 脾气好，朋友不多
   - Ⓓ 容易相处，多心   (   )

Speaking

1. Describe the personality of one of your favorite classmates.

2. Search online for three celebrities and find out the people who have influenced these celebrities in their lives. Share your findings with the class.

3. What is your personality like? What type of people do you get along with? What type of people do you find it hard to get along with?

Reading

1. Match the personality traits with the celebrities.

   A) 有礼貌
   B) 有耐心
   C) 挑剔
   D) 大方
   E) 热心
   F) 诚实
   G) 开朗
   H) 友善
   I) 细心 (xìxīn, meticulous)
   J) 容易相处
   K) 脾气好

   1) Steve Jobs
   2) Mother Teresa
   3) Barack Obama
   4) Emma Watson
   5) Jeremy Lin

2. Read the job recruitment notice and decide who among your classmates would fit the position best.

   "有耐心、有爱心、细心、友善、开朗、热心、诚实、脾气好、喜欢和小孩子一起工作。"

3. People of all professions have influence on various aspects of our society. Select the correct options to complete the sentences.

1) 警察对（　　　）影响很大。

2) 医生对（　　　）影响很大。

3) 市长对（　　　）影响很大。

4) 教师对（　　　）影响很大。

5) 总统对（　　　）影响很大。
（zǒngtǒng / president）

A) 城市的发展 (fāzhǎn / development)
B) 社会的安全 (ānquán / safety)
C) 学生的成长 (chéngzhǎng / growth)
D) 国家的前途 (qiántú / future)
E) 人们的健康

4. Read the paragraph and answer the questions.

我爸爸是一个图书馆员。他很喜欢他的工作。爸爸小时候就很喜欢看书。那时候他一有时间，就去图书馆看书。每次从图书馆回来，他都会借好多书回家来读。爸爸常常对我说，看书是很好的学习(xuéxí)，你可以认识一个人、一个国家、一段(duàn / section)历史，了解(liǎojiě / understand)一个职业(zhíyè / profession)、一个行业，学到很多你的时代(shídài / era)和社会以外的东西。

在爸爸的影响下，我也越来越喜欢看书，喜欢去图书馆，有时候还帮图书馆员整理图书。有人问我："你将来是不是想当个图书馆员？"虽然我也喜欢书，但是我其实想从事政治，当一个市长。因为我觉得做市长会影响到更多的人的生活，更有意义。

1) 爸爸的工作是什么？对我有什么影响？

_____

2) 爸爸告诉我读书的好处是什么？

_____

3) 我将来想当图书馆员吗？我将来想做什么？为什么？

_____

Writing

1. Practice writing the following characters in the correct stroke order.

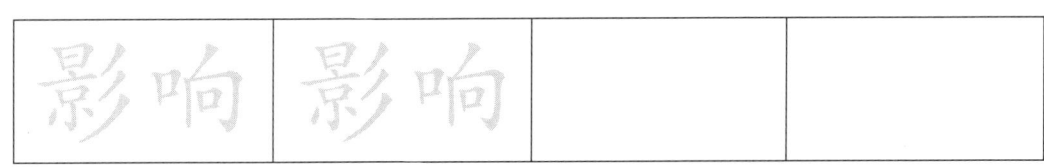

影 影 影 影 影 影 影 影 影 影 影 影 影 影 影
响 响 响 响 响 响 响 响

影响 | 影响 | 影响 | | |

受 受 受 受 受 受 受 受

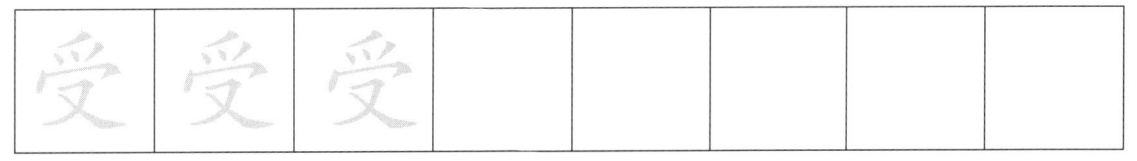

受 | 受 | 受 | 受 | | | | |

相相相相相相相相相
处处处处处

相处

性性性性性性性
格格格格格格格格格

性格

脾脾脾脾脾脾脾脾脾脾脾
气气气气

脾气

别别别别别别别

别

2. What are the professions that affect people's lives and security? List five of them.

_____

_____

_____

_____

3. What are the qualities that a nurse should have? List at least five qualities.

4. Search online and find 10 industries that have considerable influence on our environment. Write a sentence for each of them about their influence on the environment.

Example: 服装行业对环境的影响很大。

5. In college or at summer camp, you will live in a dorm with a roommate (室友). Write about your expectations for an ideal roommate, including his/her personality, interests, and hobbies. (Write at least 200 characters.)

STEP 2 HELPING THE COMMUNITY

Listening

1. Listen and choose the most appropriate response.
   - Ⓐ 没问题，我也要去医院捐血。
   - Ⓑ 我要帮儿童福利院筹款，不能跟你去。
   - Ⓒ 好，我们一起去建学校。
   - Ⓓ 妈妈让我做家务。   (   )

2. Listen to the dialog and answer the question.
   QUESTION: What does the woman plan to do during the summer?
   - Ⓐ 去中国旅游   Ⓑ 去乡村旅游
   - Ⓒ 去乡村做志愿者   Ⓓ 去中国买书、买电脑   (   )

3. Listen to the dialog and answer the question.
   QUESTION: According to the woman, why is the air quality bad?
   - Ⓐ 因为工厂排放太多废气。   Ⓑ 因为有太多电子废物。
   - Ⓒ 因为汽车的废气太多了。   Ⓓ 因为饮用水被污染了。   (   )

4. Listen and choose the most appropriate response.
   - Ⓐ 他们太自私了。   Ⓑ 他们是环境保护的志愿者。
   - Ⓒ 他们要倒垃圾。   Ⓓ 他们喜欢打扫公园。   (   )

Speaking

1. Describe the community service you would be interested in. List five types of community service that you can volunteer for.

2. In order to protect the environment, what do you want people to do and not to do? Give five suggestions. Use 叫, 让, and 请.

   Example: 请人们少用电。

3. What are the environmental problems we have to face today? List five problems using 被.

   Example: 我们的空气被污染了。

Reading

1. Match the pictures with the correct descriptions.

   (   )

   (   )

   (   )

   (   )

   (   )

Ⓐ 全球变暖　　　　　　Ⓑ 空气污染
Ⓒ 冰川融化　　　　　　Ⓓ 电子废物
Ⓔ 饮用水污染

2. Read the following passage and answer the questions by choosing the most appropriate answers.

我的一天

这个星期六，我又和芳芳一起去社区中心的敬老院帮忙。我们帮敬老院的爷爷奶奶们打扫房间、擦桌子、扫地、浇花。除了这些，我们还和他们聊天。

芳芳是一个乐于助人(lè yú zhù rén / love to help others)的好学生，每天放学以后，她都去社区中心的敬老院帮忙，她为(for)敬老院的爷爷奶奶做简单(jiǎndān / simple)的饭。要是周末有空的话，她也会去敬老院，和爷爷奶奶聊天。我受芳芳的影响很大，是她带我一起去敬老院帮忙的。

今天除了去敬老院帮忙，我们还去了社区中心做家教。芳芳周末经常去社区中心做中文家教。芳芳的父母是中国人，芳芳的中文非常好。所以，她周末有空的时候去做中文家教。受芳芳的影响，我今天也去社区中心帮忙，我的数学很好，所以，我帮社区的小学生学数学。小学生都很有礼貌，我也很有耐心。能帮助他们我非常开心。

1) 我和芳芳今天做了什么?
   Ⓐ 去了社区中心的敬老院。　Ⓑ 在社区的小学帮忙。
   Ⓒ 帮爸爸妈妈打扫屋子。　Ⓓ 跟学生聊天。　　　　　(　　)

2) 我们帮敬老院的爷爷奶奶们做了什么?
   Ⓐ 帮他们做简单的饭。
   Ⓑ 带他们去社区中心。
   Ⓒ 教他们说英文。
   Ⓓ 打扫房间、浇花,也跟他们聊天。　　　　　　　　(　　)

3) 芳芳每天放学以后做什么?
   Ⓐ 回家看爷爷奶奶。　Ⓑ 去社区中心教中文。
   Ⓒ 去敬老院帮忙。　Ⓓ 去小学教数学。　　　　　　(　　)

4) 芳芳做什么家教?为什么?
   Ⓐ 英文,因为她喜欢说英文。
   Ⓑ 数学,因为她的数学很好。
   Ⓒ 中文,因为她的中文很好。
   Ⓓ 法文,因为她会做法国菜。　　　　　　　　　　　(　　)

5) 我做什么家教?
   Ⓐ 英文。　Ⓑ 数学。
   Ⓒ 化学。　Ⓓ 中文。　　　　　　　　　　　　　　(　　)

3. Read the dialog and determine whether the following statements are true (T) or false (F).

马克:现在汽车越来越多,城市里的空气都被汽车废气污染了。

安琪:是啊,空气这么差(chā, poor),对我们的健康影响很大。

马克：除了空气污染，我们周围的环境也被污染了。

安琪：怎么说呢？

马克：我家附近的公园，每个周末都有很多人在那里野餐。但是他们吃完东西后却不收拾干净，留下很多垃圾。整个公园都被他们弄脏了。

安琪：这些人也太自私了。

马克：对，保护环境，人人有责。有时我和弟弟在公园野餐，我总会叫他把垃圾倒进垃圾桶里，保持公园的整洁。

安琪：如果每个人都像你一样，那就好了。

1) 马克觉得空气被工厂废气污染了。（　）
2) 安琪觉得空气污染对身体影响不大。（　）
3) 周末的公园很干净。（　）
4) 公园被野餐的人弄脏了。（　）
5) 马克和弟弟每次在公园野餐后，都会把地方收拾干净。（　）

Writing

1. Practice writing the following characters in the correct stroke order.

叫 叫 叫 叫 叫

叫

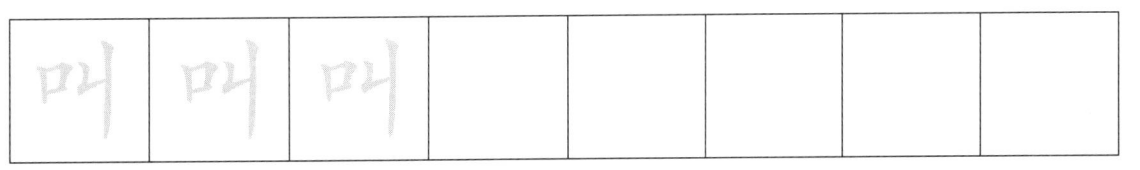

让 让 让 让 让

让

捐 捐 捐 捐 捐 捐 捐 捐 捐 捐

捐

建 建 建 建 建 建 建 建

建

被 被 被 被 被 被 被 被 被 被

被

环 环 环 环 环 环 环
境 境 境 境 境 境 境 境 境 境 境

环境

污 污 污 污 污 污
染 染 染 染 染 染 染 染

污染

2. List five types of pollution that are common in the area you live.

_____

_____

_____

_____

3. Change the following 把 - sentences into 被 - sentences.

1) 工厂把小河污染了。
         hé
         river

_____

2) 孩子把垃圾桶弄倒了。

_____

3) 我们把旅行计划做好了。
         jìhuà
         plan

_____

4) 她把电脑弄丢了。
       diū
       lose

_____

5) 他把电脑修好了。

_____

4. In a weekend designated for community-building, what are the things that you can ask a friend to do with you? Write at least five things. Use 叫, 让, or 请 in your sentences.

Example: 我要请朋友和我一起去捐血。

STEP 3 CREATING A BETTER LIFE

Listening

1. Listen to the dialog and answer the question.
   QUESTION: What eco-friendly habit did the man suggest?
   - Ⓐ 把垃圾分类
   - Ⓑ 自备购物袋。
   - Ⓒ 少吃肉。
   - Ⓓ 多坐公交车。   (   )

2. Listen to the dialog and choose the most logical explanation.
   - Ⓐ 你这样做既省电又环保。
   - Ⓑ 你不可以吃这么多肉。
   - Ⓒ 吃太多肉对身体不好。
   - Ⓓ 你以后不要拿(take)这么多。吃不完多浪费啊！   (   )

3. Listen and choose the most logical response to the statement.
   - Ⓐ 我不喜欢骑车，我要走路。
   - Ⓑ 我上班开车要二十分钟。
   - Ⓒ 你应该把你的垃圾分类。
   - Ⓓ 二氧化碳会让地球很热。   (   )

4. Listen and choose the most logical response to the question.
   - Ⓐ 我们家又买了一辆新车。
   - Ⓑ 路上的车辆太多了，排出了太多的废气。
   - Ⓒ 北京的天气热极了。
   - Ⓓ 你知道吗，北京把很多工厂都搬走了。   (   )

Speaking

1. In the U.S., people tend to eat more meat than people in China. Think about how meat gets to your plate and what it entails. Discuss why eating vegetables is environmentally friendly.

2. Imagine your family plans to buy a car. From the perspective of protecting the environment, what would you suggest for the size and shape and why?

3. How can a family help protect the environment in the following situations? Use ……的时候 and 应该.

    Example: Have dinner in a restaurant
    在餐馆吃晚饭的时候，我们应该少吃肉，多吃菜。

    1) Go to a nearby park
    2) Shop in a supermarket
    3) Watch TV at home

4. Which leisure activities are environmentally friendly and why? State five of them that you should do during weekends to help protect the environment, and explain why the activity will help the environment.

    Example: 周末，我们应该去外边打球，因为在外边打球不用电，很环保。

Reading

1. Read the following environmentally friendly measures and mark a check for those that you often practice and a cross for those that you plan to practice in the future.

    1) 节约用水 （　）
    2) 随手关灯 （　）
    3) 电池回收 (huíshōu, recycle) （　）
    4) 垃圾分类 （　）
    5) 饭菜打包 （　）
    6) 步行上学 （　）
    7) 使用楼梯 （　）
    8) 不用一次性餐具 （　）
    9) 不用瓶装水 （　）
    10) 不用塑料袋 （　）

2. Read the following practices and check those which are environmentally friendly.

1) 我们应该少吃肉，多吃菜，因为生产(shēngchǎn, produce)和加工(jiāgōng, process)肉会用很多的电。( )

2) 我们不要浪费水，这样就可以节约能源。( )

3) 我们可以多用一次性的瓶装水，因为塑料瓶是可以回收的。( )

4) 我们在家里要少用电灯和空调，这样可以节约能源。( )

5) 电池是垃圾，可以扔(rēng, throw)到垃圾桶里。( )

3. Fill in the blanks using the options provided.

今天我们的生活很方便，但是也给1( )带来了伤害。比如，现在人们常常会开车去别的地方。结果，汽车的废气就会带来2( )。再如，人们不再用手洗衣服，而是用洗衣机和烘干机。它们给我们带来了方便，但是很浪费水和电，这样就加大了3( )的使用和二氧化碳的排放。我们平时用的电器，都是在消耗能源。结果空气中的二氧化碳4( )，地球大气5( )，冰山融化也6( )。为了下一代有一个美好的环境，我们7( )节约用水，用电，坚持垃圾8( )，不要浪费粮食，少吃肉类。做一个环境保护的9( )。

- Ⓐ 应该
- Ⓑ 越来越热
- Ⓒ 志愿者
- Ⓓ 空气污染
- Ⓔ 能源
- Ⓕ 越来越快
- Ⓖ 环境
- Ⓗ 越来越多
- Ⓘ 分类

4. Read the text and determine whether the following statements are true (T) or false (F).

各位同学，(gè wèi / every)

大家好！

每年一次的绿杯比赛又要开始了。请每位同学注意节约用电，及时关灯。人不在房间里的时候，要把空调和电风扇也关上。我们会在每个星期一发电邮给大家，公布每个宿舍的成绩。十月十五号我们会给第一名的宿舍发奖，奖品是冰淇淋。

(kāishǐ - start; zhùyì - take note of; jíshí - promptly; kōngtiáo - air-conditioner; gōngbù - announce; sùshè - dorm; chéngjì - results; jiǎngpǐn - prize)

环境连着你我他，节约能源靠大家！欢迎你参加绿杯环保节能大赛！

(lián - link; kào - depend on; jiénéng - save energy)

学生会 (student council)
二零一四年九月十五日

1) The Green Cup contest is for saving energy. ( )
2) The Green Cup contest is held every month. ( )
3) Only the lights and fans should be turned off when people are not in the room. ( )
4) Every Monday there will be an email to everyone announcing the best performing dormitory. ( )
5) The main purpose of this text is to educate students on how to save energy. ( )

Writing

1. Practice writing the following characters in the correct stroke order.

节 节 节 节 节
约 约 约 约 约 约

节约 | 节约 | 节约 | | |

减 减 减 减 减 减 减 减 减 减 减
少 少 少 少

减少 | 减少 | 减少 | | |

浪 浪 浪 浪 浪 浪 浪 浪 浪 浪
费 费 费 费 费 费 费 费 费

浪费 | 浪费 | 浪费 | | |

当 当 当 当 当 当

当 | 当 | 当 | 当 | | | | |

离 离 离 离 离 离 离 离 离 离
开 开 开 开

离开 | 离开 | 离开 | | |

LESSON 10 BEING A GLOBAL CITIZEN

2. What are the things that we should and should not do to protect the environment? Write five ideas using 应该, and five using 不要/不应该.

_____

_____

_____

_____

_____

3. What should you do at the following times to protect the environment?

> *Example:* When leaving the room
> 当我要离开房间的时候，我应该把灯关上。

1) After watching TV

_____

2) When brushing your teeth

_____

3) When going to school

_____

4) Before throwing out the garbage

_____

5) When buying groceries

_____

4. Write an essay on the topic of 我是一个地球公民, focusing on environmental issues and how to protect the environment. Try to use new vocabulary and new structures introduced in this lesson when appropriate. (Write at least 200 characters.)

REVIEW 2 (Lessons 6 – 10)

Listening

1. Listen to the dialog and choose the most appropriate answer for the question.
   QUESTION: What is Anqi trying to say?
   Ⓐ She is good at writing letters.
   Ⓑ She doesn't communicate via email.
   Ⓒ People nowadays often communicate using the Internet.
   Ⓓ She prefers to do online chatting.   (   )

2. Listen to the dialog and choose the most appropriate answer for the question.
   QUESTION: Why is Mark tired?
   Ⓐ He sleeps late because he often plays games and watches movies.
   Ⓑ His roommate loves singing and practices singing every night.
   Ⓒ His roommate often sleeps 5 or 6 hours every night.
   Ⓓ His roommate sleeps late because he is playing games, watching movies,
      and singing, all of which affect Mark's sleep.   (   )

3. Listen to the dialog and choose the most appropriate answer for the question.
   QUESTION: What does Fangfang need to do to take care of Harley?
   Ⓐ She needs to feed it three times a day.
   Ⓑ She needs to walk it three times a day.
   Ⓒ She needs to go to New York for a meeting.
   Ⓓ She needs to feed and walk it three times a day.   (   )

4. Listen to the dialog and choose the most appropriate answer for the question.
   QUESTION: Which statement is not correct?
   Ⓐ Tomorrow is the weekend.
   Ⓑ The woman plans to clean the community center.
   Ⓒ The gentleman wants to help out with the cleaning.
   Ⓓ The woman wants the gentleman to help with the cleaning.   (   )

5. Listen to the dialog and choose the most appropriate answer for the question.
QUESTION: Why does the man refuse to get the woman a coke?
(Check all that apply.)
- **A** He wants her to drink some healthy drinks. ( )
- **B** He thinks coke is not healthy. ( )
- **C** She has drunk too much coke today. ( )
- **D** He thinks coke tastes great. ( )

Speaking

1. Imagine you have a friend who is not in good health because of his unhealthy habits of eating fast food and lack of exercise. Prepare a speech giving your suggestions on how to stay healthy as well as what is good for his/her health.
(Structures recommended are: 对……有好处；应该；虽然…但是…；如果…就…）

2. Nowadays students' leisure activities are greatly influenced by technology. Work with a partner on your plans for the weekend. Have a short debate on outdoor activity vs. online entertainment.
(Structures recommended are: 要是…就…；虽然…但是…；应该；一边…一边…；可以）

3. Talk about the environmental issues in your community and what else you should do to protect the environment.
(Structures recommended are: 不但…而且…；被；把；如果…就…；应该）

4. What would you like to do in the future? Why? Does anyone play a role in this decision? Also, talk about what you want to do to change your community while working in that field.
(Structures recommended are: 打算；因为…所以…；受；让；除了…以外）

5. Working with a partner, talk about each other's personality and how each of you can get along better with others.
(Structures recommended are: 不但…而且；因为…所以；应该；如果…就）

Reading

1. Read the doctor's prescription and answer the questions in Chinese.

姓名：王东明

年龄(niánlíng)：15岁

性别(xìngbié)：男

处方(chǔfāng)日期：2015年9月25日

药品：感冒伤风片

用法：口服(kǒufú)一日三次，一次一片到两片。凉开水服下。

另(lìng)：适量(shìliàng)多喝水，不吃辛辣(xīnlà)，多休息。

医生：李天乐

1) 王东明得了什么病？

_____

2) 医生让他吃什么药？一天几次，一次几片？

_____

3) 除了吃药，医生还让王晓明做什么？不做什么？

_____

2. Read the instructions below and number the tasks in the correct order.

> "请大家先到教室，我们要把清洁工作先分给每个同学。然后同学们一起到社区中心取工具(gōngjù tool)，每人一个。拿了工具以后，我们再去老人之家帮忙打扫卫生。打扫完以后，请同学们把工具还回到社区之家。最后每个同学要回到教室，拿书包，放学回家。"

(　　) 回教室，拿书包，放学回家

(　　) 去社区中心，取工具

(　　) 把工具还回社区中心

(　　) 到老人之家打扫卫生

(　　) 到教室，分工

3. Read the following environmental protection slogans and draw a brief cartoon to explain them.

A) 地球(earth)是我家，环保靠(kào, depend on)大家。

B) 节约用水，人人有责(responsibility)。

C) 多种一棵(kē)树，就是给地球添(tiān, add)一份(fèn)爱心(àixīn, love)。

D) 请随手关灯。

E) 关心(show concern)环境，不用一次性餐具。

F) 回收(recycle)利用(lìyòng, make use of)，变(biàn, to change)废为利。

4. Read this person's daily schedule in the summer and check the suggestions that you think the person should follow.

上午10:30	起床
中午11:30	吃早饭（炸鸡、炸薯条、可乐、冰淇淋）
下午1:00 - 4:30	玩电脑游戏
下午5:00 - 8:00	看电影
晚上8:30	吃晚饭（汉堡包、炸薯条、可乐、蛋糕）
晚上9:00 - 12:00	看网上新闻、写博客、玩电脑游戏
半夜1:00	睡觉

Suggestions:
1) 他应该在晚上十一点以前睡觉。 ( )
2) 他应该少吃油炸食品。 ( )
3) 他应该多看新闻。 ( )
4) 他应该少玩电脑游戏。 ( )
5) 他应该多做户外(huwài, outdoor)活动。 ( )

5. Read the passage about Mark's uncle and answer the questions in Chinese.

> 我叔叔是一名环保工作者(zhě, -er, -ist)，他每天观测(guāncè, observe and predict)空气中的污染指数(zhǐshù, index)，把空气质量(zhìliàng)报告(bàogào, report)给环保局。叔叔说自己的性格比较内向(nèixiàng, introverted)，不太喜欢与人打交道(dǎ jiāodào, make contact with)，所以比较适合(shìhé, suited for)做观测空气污染的工作。
>
> 其实(qíshí, actually)叔叔的爱好很多，他不但喜欢户外运动，而且喜欢网络和高科技产品(gāo kējì chǎnpǐn, high tech product)。如果有时间，叔叔就去爬山，拍(pāi, take)漂亮的风景照片(fēngjǐng zhàopiàn, scenery photo)。回到家里他就在网上写博客，发照片。
>
> 很多人都是他的博客的爱好者。每到一个地方，叔叔都会细心(xìxīn, careful)地观察(guānchá, observe)当地(local)的环境情况(qíngkuàng, condition)，还会帮助清理(qīnglǐ, clear)旅游者留下(liúxià, leave behind)的垃圾。他常说关心身边的环境是每个人应该做的。

1) What is Mark's uncle's profession?

_____

2) What is his uncle's personality like?

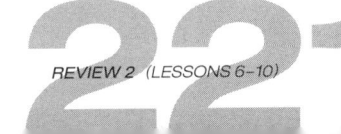

_____

3) What hobbies does his uncle have?

___

4) What does his uncle believe when it comes to protecting the environment?

___

Writing

1. Give at least five examples for each of the following:
   1) Household chores you can help with

   ___

   ___

   2) Professions you find interesting

   ___

   ___

   3) Activities you can do online

   ___

   ___

   4) Healthy foods you can think of

   ___

   ___

5) Environmentally friendly habits in people's daily lives

_____

_____

2. Write a brief description of a celebrity who has contributed greatly to his/her country and/or the world using 在……方面，不仅…还…. (Write at least 50 characters.)

_____

_____

_____

_____

3. Imagine you are trying to help the elderly in the community use technology. Write instructions for the tasks below. You may use an English-Chinese dictionary to find words you don't know.
   (Structures recommended are: 先…再…然后…最后…; 要是…就…; 把)

   1) How to read news online

   _____

   2) How to send text messages using a cellphone

   _____

   3) How to write an email using a computer

   _____

4) How to watch a movie online using an iPad

5) How to find the weather forecast from a website

4. Write five habits that are good for your health.

> *Example:* 每天刷牙两次，睡觉前一次，起床后一次。

5. Research online to find out what difference it makes to turn off the lights for an hour. Write a short poster message to your school on the benefits of saving energy. (Write at least 50 characters.)